WE'RE
GONNA NEED
CAKE

Celebrating Authentic Leadership in a Messy World

• • •

WE'RE GONNA NEED CAKE

VALERIE GARCIA

PAGE TWO

Cataloguing in publication information
is available from Library and Archives Canada.
ISBN 978-1-77458-448-4 (paperback)
ISBN 978-1-77458-449-1 (ebook)

Page Two
pagetwo.com

Edited by Emily Schultz
Copyedited by Indu Singh
Cover, interior design, and illustrations by Jennifer Lum

valeriegarcia.com

CONTENTS

THE LIES WE'VE BEEN TOLD

• • •

REMEMBER A time when I was excited about work. I liked the idea of projects and people and even the thought of meetings thrilled me. Work always seemed like the grown-up version of the first day of school—fresh school supplies, newly sharpened pencils, and a cool new backpack.

After I entered the workforce, however, particularly the corporate world, the romance of it soon wore off. I heard words like "hustle," "grind," and "crush." I learned about key performance indicators (KPIs) and expense reports and similar unsexy things. Meetings became something I hated, and "You've got mail" was certainly not as fun as it was portrayed by Meg Ryan.

All in all, it quickly started to feel like something I had to do rather than something I got to do.

I was raised to believe that emotions are weaknesses. "Stop being so emotional" was something I was told regularly. And the corporate world seemed to reinforce this message time and time again.

At work, everyone seemed to follow these unwritten rules of professionalism *(with their unspoken, but clearly implied, subtext)*:

Dress for the job you want, not the one you have.
(You should always want more than you have.
Keep hustling.)

Keep it together in front of the staff.
(No one can ever see those normal human emotions or
they'll think you can't do your job. Suck it up.)

Leave your personal life at the door.
(Stuff all the hard things you are dealing with in a box,
please and thanks. This isn't the place for that.)

Winners never quit.
(How dare you be tired! You can't possibly say no
to anything, ever.)

Never let them see you sweat.
(God forbid you act human.)

Just keep your head down and do your job.
(Hustle. Grind.)

But the most important message was this: *Keep your emotions out of it.* This was the crappiest of all the unwritten rules because as humans, we are guaranteed to fail at this one.

Those rules shaped the way I showed up at work and ultimately how I led others, until one day when my life fell apart. And that is when I realized that all those unwritten rules were lies. I didn't need them, and they weren't making me a better leader.

Lying seems like one of those things that most of us agree is wrong. And yet, as adults, we tend to live by and retell the same lies that we have been told over and over.

I was a VP leading an international team, and my personal life fell apart. I fell into a deep depression while continuing to show up at work, get on stages, and tell people how to run their businesses. All the while, I was lying to myself and everyone around me. I didn't tell anyone that I was struggling and grieving and messy.

I was trying to follow those stupid rules that said my emotions couldn't play a role in my work, and as a result, my work suffered. My mental health suffered. My team suffered. But most of all—I suffered.

I wasn't showing up to work as a complete human, and it was impacting my performance, my leadership, and ultimately keeping me from finding joy in my work.

So I decided to ditch the rules.

I told the truth about how I was feeling. I learned to bravely ask for help. I showed up with both fear and curiosity in my leadership approach. I put my mess on display for those around me. I stopped leaving my emotions out of my work and started leading *with* them. And I learned lessons that changed my life.

There are a lot of business books out there. Books that will teach you how to hustle and grind and crush it at work. *This is not that book.*

This book is about being a hot mess and showing up anyway. About the totally normal and natural human emotions that we all feel every day, and how they are actually our superpower and not our downfall.

But mostly, this book is about unlearning all the lies we've been told our entire lives about what authentic leadership actually looks like.

Maybe you've also lost your excitement for your work. Maybe instead of newly sharpened pencils and fresh notebooks, work is starting to feel more like dirty gym socks and getting dumped by Jason the day before homecoming. (That happened. I'm totally over it.)

This book is for you.

Maybe you have lost sight of what real authenticity can look and feel like at work. Or maybe you've bought into the lie that authenticity means you have to stuff all your messy humanness into a box and leave it at the door.

This book is for you.

Or, like the past-me, maybe you are exhausted by the endless hustle and grind. Maybe you are looking for a way to be both a better leader and a better human, without the constant pressure to be something or someone you are not.

Then this book is *especially* for you.

I clawed my way from failure to joy—having spent decades in a corporate hustle culture, working with some of the biggest brands and speaking on some of the biggest stages, while struggling with anxiety, depression, and burn-out. I learned my lessons the hard way. My entire world had to come crashing down for me to recognize that there was a better way.

• • •

This book is about unlearning all the lies we've been told our entire lives about what authentic leadership actually looks like.

• • •

Every day I speak with leaders who are "putting on a face" for their team. They desperately want permission to be honest and real about the struggles they face at home and at work. They attend conferences and hire coaches to help them become more authentic, but they are still stuck in the same patterns that keep them unhappy and exhausted. I want you to experience the relief that will come from getting real with the people you serve and lead.

Success alone is fine. But creating a career filled with joy and authenticity is richer than you can imagine. It gives your job purpose and meaning, but also so much more to celebrate than just hitting a sales goal or accomplishing a KPI. And there is no joy more worthy of celebrating than being able to be exactly you.

No matter where you are in your journey to joyful work, this book provides a road map through the mess. Each chapter helps you navigate the emotions that can and should make you more effective and joyful at work. The roadblocks will help you identify what might be keeping you from moving forward, and the exercises will prompt you to unlearn the lies you've been told (and the ones you keep telling yourself).

Learning to navigate all the roadblocks and show up fully despite our mess—that is what will make us the best, most effective, and most joyful leaders, employees, business owners, and humans that we can be.

This book is about messy moments at work. But it's also about joyful moments. (And all the moments in between!) In my experience, all of those events should be celebrated.

Cake is something that I have always associated with the break room at work. There was cake to celebrate birthdays and births and promotions, but there was also cake for retirements and goodbyes and funerals. Life and work are both filled with a mashup of joy and pain, failure and triumph. We should celebrate the lessons that come with all of them.

It's possible to find joy at work, even when things are messy. It's possible to be a truly authentic leader, even when you are messy. And the messier life gets, friends, the more *we're gonna need cake.*

1
THE MESS
DITCH THE CAFETERIA TRAY

● ● ●

To only share the wonderful is not real.
It's not human.
It's inhumane.
No one wants smoke and mirrors.

MARC PIMSLER, author, therapist, coach,
and executive director of the International Society
for Experiential Professionals (ISEP)

WAS SUPPOSED to get on stage that morning. It was an annual meeting with hundreds of our company's leaders, owners, and stakeholders.

I was the hype girl that day. It was my job to outline all our wins and plans for the year going forward. I had a slide deck of charts and graphs and positive numbers. I was the one who was supposed to convince everyone that we were on the right track and show up with a smile on my face.

But instead, I was in a utility closet, sobbing.

A few days prior, a colleague I didn't know well had asked me to lunch. While we were sitting there, eating our salads, she started to cry. "My husband is cheating on me," she said. "My life is a mess, my job is a mess, I am a mess. But I have been watching you and you seem to have it all together. I want to know what your secret is."

I don't remember what I said to her that day. I only remember sitting there silently screaming inside, because I was in the exact same boat.

My husband had left me. A nearly twenty-year relationship over, without warning. For two years I had been battling deep grief and depression, struggling to even get out of bed in the mornings. At work I felt I was not being an effective leader or a good teammate. I was barely present.

But I just kept going to work and acting like everything was fine. I hadn't told a soul that my entire world had crashed down around my ears. I hadn't even told my family.

I was a hot, hot mess. How could anyone look at me and think I had it all together?

And that morning, when I was supposed to get on stage and once again paste on a smile and talk about how great everything was and how well my department was performing, I was instead sobbing in the utility closet.

Because I just couldn't bring myself to fake it one more time.

Most of us operate with a set of expectations around keeping our personal lives and work lives separate. We operate by those unwritten rules that everyone seems to know:

Don't be too emotional.
Leave your personal life at the door.
Winners never quit.
Fake it 'til you make it.
Just keep your head down and do your job.

And that day as I was falling apart right there in the utility closet, I thought to myself: *How can I be this person? How can I manage people and be a mess? How can I get on stage and be a mess? How can I coach other people and be a mess?* It felt like I was breaking all the rules.

And let me tell you, I like rules. I've always been one of those eaters where my peas don't touch my carrots.

My life had always been like one of those cafeteria trays. You know the ones. Those rectangle trays that kept your applesauce from touching your pizza. I kept nice, neat dividers between all my worries, keeping everything in its tidy little square, never touching and never mixing. My marriage struggles couldn't touch my management skills, which couldn't touch my aging parents, and so on.

I had this constant internal voice asking, *What if they see my mess? What if they think there must be something wrong with me?*

So, I stuffed all my emotions in a drawer and pretended they didn't exist. I continued to show up at work feeling heavy, exhausted, scared, isolated, and overwhelmed—but pretending I was winning and fine and hustling.

To the outside eye, I was crushing it. I was speaking on the biggest stages, crisscrossing the world working with some of the biggest brands. I had my name in lights and my peas and carrots nice and tidy. Hashtag blessed!

But I was a mess. And I know I'm not alone.

The truth is, life isn't a cafeteria tray. Life is like a Thanksgiving dinner plate where everything is all piled on top of each other, smooshed together, and covered in gravy.

We're all messy.

You might have to take a pill every day just to get out of bed. You might be in the middle of a divorce. Your kids may be in therapy. Your career might be in shambles. You might be figuring out how to deal with aging parents. You might be depending on credit cards to make ends meet.

We are basically running our work lives like those cafeteria trays, trying like hell to keep everything neat and divided. In large part, that is because of the stories and unwritten rules that are on a loop in our own heads.

We're not allowed to be both leaders *and* a mess.
We're not allowed to be employees *and* a mess.
We're not allowed to be successful *and* a mess.

But the morning I found myself in that utility closet, I made a decision to start telling the truth. And when I did that, everything changed. People showed up for me in ways I never expected. Others started telling me their own stories. My employees opened up to me. I became a more effective leader. And I started getting hired to tell the truth.

. . .

We are basically running our work lives

like those cafeteria trays, trying like hell

to keep everything neat and divided.

. . .

It was such a relief to realize I didn't have to have it all together all of the time. Pretending was really just being numb—blocking out all the natural and healthy emotions that made me a whole human. And numbness was exhausting.

For years, I'd been listening to others talk about authenticity on stages. I had heard gurus and speakers talk about *showing up as your authentic self.* But I think that most people confuse that for their pretty peas-and-carrots Instagram version.

Authenticity isn't the absence of mess. Authenticity only happens when you navigate through the mess and unlearn all of those unwritten rules that are keeping you from telling the truth.

We often think that the opposite of grief or sadness or numbness is joy. But the opposite of numbness is real authenticity. Authenticity is allowing yourself to feel and embody all the things—the joy and the grief and the mess. It's admitting that we feel it all. Because feeling it all makes us better humans and better leaders. In order to be truly authentic at work, we have to show up with all of it.

The writer Scott Monty says, "Authenticity represents who we are, not what we do. It is more of a state of being rather than a skill—it's something that has to be part of your personality rather than something that can be taught."

I think Monty is spot on with the first part of that quote—authenticity *is* who we are, and it is a state of being. But I disagree with the last part—I think we can learn to do the things that allow us to be more human at work. And it starts with learning to embrace the mess.

Taking time to celebrate the things that make us human, real, and messy is a critical part of leadership. Those cake moments (whether we're in the break room with actual cake, or on a Slack channel, sharing laughter and levity) are opportunities to just be, instead of being expected to perform.

A recent study by BeYourselfAtWork, an organization committed to creating a more human workplace, found that just 16 percent of people surveyed feel that they can bring their real selves to their workplace. However, research shows that when people are themselves at work, their performance can be positively impacted by up to 85 percent, and 97 percent say they perform better when they can be themselves at work.

Encouraging authenticity isn't just a recipe for great leadership; it's a solid business strategy as well.

. . .

DITCH THE TRAY (OR NOT)

What does it mean to be messy?

I get that you might be wondering this at this point. And I get that it's not conducive to great work to be sobbing in a utility closet all the time. So, what does it really look like to be messy at work?

The myth is that being messy just means being "too emotional."

In truth, emotions play a critical role in our lives. Emotions help us take action, survive, avoid danger, make decisions, and understand others. They also help other people to understand *us*.

Humans are complex social and emotional beings. Our well-being depends on learning how to communicate our needs to each other and managing our emotions in healthy ways. Also, we are born with an instinct for forming social connections. This is how we have survived both saber-toothed tigers and Facebook.

Being messy means more than simply showing our emotions. It means being honest about our struggles instead of pretending they don't exist. And it means letting those struggles and emotions weave their way into the work we do, instead of trying to keep them neat and tidy and divided.

Being messy is true authenticity.

Katie Burke, the chief people officer at HubSpot, defines this kind of authenticity as "not having to put on a mask to come to work and not feeling like who I am personally and professionally are at odds with one another."

People often assume authenticity and vulnerability mean sharing everything about yourself. I called Katie to ask how she approaches authenticity when working as a leader in an organization with over seventy-five hundred employees.

Katie replied, "I think sometimes when it comes to authenticity, people think that means you're always vulnerable or you're always a feeler." She added, "It's actually about knowing when you feel comfortable bringing those elements of yourself to the table, and that changes daily based on the situation you're in. I like challenging the assumption—sometimes authenticity is vulnerability, and sometimes authenticity is being like, I can't go there today."

At HubSpot, a key element of their regular team meeting is check-ins where team members share how they are feeling—and the words "good" and "busy" are not allowed. Part of the follow-up is a green card or red card exercise. Is it okay with people to check in with you, or not?

"And it's okay to call a red card, like, I'm just not in a position to follow up," Katie says. "I think for the people on my team who are empaths, myself included, it can be hard to be like, it's not actually okay for me to follow up with you because that's your call. And I'm not gonna lie, I wrestle with that. But I think part of the balance of true authenticity is creating space for both."

Creating space for both. At the same time. Space for the cafeteria tray and the Thanksgiving dinner. *That is true authenticity.*

• • •

THE COST OF INAUTHENTICITY

HubSpot is one of the many organizations that have shifted to embrace the new reality of hybrid and remote work. Along with that shift has come a laundry list of new leadership challenges.

How do we manage people we rarely see in person? How do we check in with people who are struggling? How do we ensure that our teams are operating efficiently when many or all of their members are working in isolation? And how do we make sure no one is falling through the cracks?

Statistics tell us that more than 280 million people in the world struggle with depression. In fact, in the US, more than four in ten adults say that they lack companionship, their relationships are not meaningful, and they feel isolated from others. In Canada, those results were one in four.

The World Health Organization calls social isolation and loneliness a "priority public health problem."

At the same time, we are experiencing a phenomenon dubbed the Great Resignation, which is leading to a large number of people reshuffling roles, jobs, and careers all at once, destabilizing teams and organizations en masse.

And ironically, the loudest debate is perhaps around the term "quiet quitting"—the idea that millions of people are not going above and beyond at work, but instead just meeting the basics of their job description—a concept that is spreading virally. According to Gallup research, this could describe more than 50 percent of American workers and cost the world $7.8 trillion in lost productivity, which is equal to 11 percent of global GDP.

Gallup found that while many organizations are shifting their culture and promising to accommodate these new realities, "your employer brand is only able to get the best of your people when it's an *authentic* representation of reality—what employees experience in your work culture every day."

Authentic. Real.

For years, companies and organizations have gotten away with inconsistencies in what they say about their values and what those values look like in the wild. It was easier to do this before social media, but these days, people are watching and talking.

Furthermore, we've been perpetuating this idea that leaders and employees have to compartmentalize their real lives from their work lives, and it's eating away at our souls, causing isolation, loneliness, and, ultimately, resignations.

This level of inauthenticity isn't sustainable.

Katie Burke says she's starting to see cracks in this long-held facade: "I think one tiny silver lining of the pandemic was that you did drop the ball, right? You had kids, pets, partners, and roommates, coming in and interrupting. I think it actually did a world of good to embrace the imperfection of a Zoom background or the Wi-Fi dropping out. It normalizes the humanity of things."

She continues, "What's interesting on the recruiting side is that so many companies have forced people to go back to the office. They've almost been like, that was cute but now pull it back. But one of the things that we're really emphasizing is we're keeping that part, whether you're in the office or whether you're at home, we're keeping that normalcy of just being human. That is more important than ever as it relates to retaining people. People know you can probably always go somewhere else and get more money or a higher title. There's always going to be a company in the world that does that.

"One of the things we're learning is that for people, as they navigate any sort of milestone—and it can be good things, like buying a house or having a child, but it could also be tough stuff, like a divorce, not getting a job you wanted, going through a breakup—having a more human workplace and creating space for authenticity is more likely to retain people as we grow and scale, and I think that's super important and valuable."

The cost of inauthenticity is real. And the benefits of an authentic, messy workplace are obvious. So, why does this continue to be something we struggle with?

This is where the lies come in.

. . .

WHERE WE GO WRONG

As a young employee in the corporate world, I made a ton of mistakes. Thinking of some of the ways I messed up still makes me feel embarrassed.

Like the time I asked my very first boss for the afternoon off to attend an interview for a new job. (Honesty is the best policy, right? *Yikes*.) Or the time I was asked to fax something by a person who was standing next to the fax machine, and I replied, "Are your fingers broken?" (I could die, y'all. I could die.)

But some of my worst mistakes impacted me in bigger ways. I was passed over for promotions or projects because I didn't speak up for myself or negotiate for my own skills. I missed out on critical mentorship because I didn't ask for the help I needed. And I spent years working twelve-hour days, seven days a week, because I didn't know how to put healthy boundaries in place.

I'm not sure at what point I started believing that I couldn't speak up, ask for help, or say no... but those lies shaped decades of my career in negative ways. And it took years to unlearn them.

According to Katie, I'm not alone. "I think the biggest lie that I had to unlearn is that being a female executive is about being all things to all people," she says. "I think that there is an expectation that you mentor and sponsor more than anyone else, especially your male counterparts. That being a great female executive is about being available to any woman on the planet who wants mentorship, sponsorship, help, or advice. There is this lie that there's only one way to do it, that there is one prototype of what being a female executive is or could be."

Where do these lies come from? And why do we keep telling ourselves and others that they are true?

I am going to say the hard thing: I think we do this more to ourselves than anything. Did anyone at any point tell me I had to work eighty-hour weeks to be considered a valuable team member? No. I told myself that I had to outperform everyone to prove myself. Did anyone tell me I should avoid asking for help? No. I didn't want to appear stupid or not great at my job.

Katie assured me that those self-lies about asking for help are real. "This is a really hard one. I think it's especially hard for female leaders. I think we treat women who ask for help differently than we do male leaders in the workplace, which I do think makes it doubly hard, and I think it's even harder for women of color. My first two years as our chief people officer, I was armored up and I was scheduled up. I was like, there's no room in the schedule, but I will meet with anyone. I didn't feel like I could say no to anything because my imposter syndrome was so real."

She elaborated: "If you were to tap me on the shoulder, I would jump because I was so tightly wound. Don't drop a ball. Don't mess things up, that sort of thing. So I would certainly ask for help on things like, 'Hey, I'm still learning this role.' And I would ask external leaders for advice and counsel, but I certainly wouldn't say, 'I'm not sure I'm doing this job well and can someone help me out or give me advice here.'"

Of course, it's sometimes difficult to ask. Katie continued, "It is easier to ask for help when you are in a junior role than when you're in the senior seat. I think it's easy to say that people respect that, but harder to actually do. That is something I'm still learning and unlearning. It also matters what you're asking for. Asking for advice to get unstuck is actually pretty easy for me. Saying I'm really lost and this is a big mess, and truly dropping your guard . . . I think that is harder."

And there's the rub. Dropping our guard. Looking lost. *Being messy.*

What if we made that the new leadership standard? What if we stopped telling ourselves that we have to armor up and schedule up and instead told ourselves, and those around us, that we can mess up, call a time-out, and ask for what we need?

But how do we change decades of beliefs and untruths that shape our workplaces? And how do we recreate a reality where emotions aren't the bad guys but instead are the missing pieces that bring us all together?

As I pondered these questions more, I started to realize that what I'd been missing all these years was a manual. A guide to navigating the mess and bringing my whole self to my work. A road map to help us include all the emotions that come with complex work situations—not to mention how to become more joyful at work while avoiding the big roadblocks that usually trip us up.

And that, my friends, is how I created and developed The Authenticity Map—a simple guide to finding your most real and joyful you at work.

● ● ●

THE AUTHENTICITY MAP

There are no shortcuts on this map. You have to feel all the feels to get to your destination.

You'll also notice that this map never really leads you *out* of the mess. Instead, it helps you navigate *through* it. While failure and fear are part of the mess, the good news is that so are confidence and joy.

If we want to be authentic leaders, we have to show up within the mess and help those on our team unlearn the lies that are holding them back.

THE AUTHENTICITY MAP

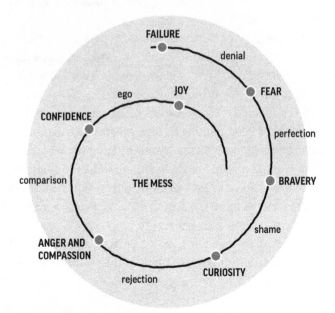

Even though this map starts with failure, I want to be very clear that the anxiety, depression, and grief that landed me in that utility closet were not failures.

This journey begins with failure because it's often a failure or a screwup that puts us in a dark hole and robs us of our joy. But depression wasn't my failure. I failed by keeping it all bottled up and pretending everything was fine. I failed at truth-telling and authenticity.

We have to stop shoving our mess in a drawer and instead make our mess our superpower. We have to show up even when we are messy ourselves so that ultimately we can do better and more meaningful work.

But first, we have to unlearn all those unwritten rules we've been telling ourselves and others. We have to replace that internal script with new rules:

We can and should ask for help.
We don't have to have it all figured out.
We are not for everyone.
We can be messy *and* be leaders.

For the cynics who are reading this, I see you. (I can cynic with the best of them.) You might be thinking that this is a bunch of woo that has nothing to do with your job. You might be convinced that you are fine, you have it all together, and nothing that bad has happened to you. You may believe that this really doesn't apply to you. You may even be asking, "Why do I want to work with leaders or employees who are messy?"

. . .

We have to stop shoving

our mess in a drawer and instead

make our mess our superpower.

. . .

The truth is, everyone is messy. Seriously, find me someone who's not. And even if they're not admitting it, chances are good they're heading for a breakdown in the utility closet. Because that was me. I was there.

I also would have said I wasn't messy. I also believed I had it all together. But I didn't. And neither do you.

The goal is not to operate in a state of numbness. It's to live in (and lead with) a state of joy. If we truly want to be authentic at work—showing up as ourselves and owning our emotions—we have to figure out how to navigate through the mess.

Navigating through the mess always starts with the messiest part, and I was most definitely in the messiest part that day in that closet.

I had to learn that if I wanted to get to joy, I had to walk the whole path. But we have to start at the beginning: by acknowledging the mess and unlearning the lies.

SELF-ASSESSMENT
• • •

What Do You Need to Unlearn?
- In what areas of your work are you being inauthentic because of past patterns?
- How are the people you lead being held back by these patterns?
- What do you have the potential to improve in your work if you are more authentic?

Get Started
How do you really want to feel at work? How do you really want to show up and bring your best *you* to the work that you do? It's difficult to navigate any map if you don't know your ultimate

destination. Before you move forward, take the time to identify the emotions you want to associate with your work, and how you want your work to make you feel.

CELEBRATE!

As I said in the Introduction, celebrations aren't reserved only for big things. This is where the idea of cake comes in—whether it's an actual cake or just marking an accomplishment. We often take time to celebrate big wins or accomplishments, but we should celebrate the small stuff too! It's allowed. You don't have to save celebration (or cake!) for a special occasion. You don't have to earn it. Took one step? Celebrate! Took ten? Celebrate! Celebrate all the things!

Identify a time in the past when you were authentic. When you felt your most *you*. At that moment did you have everything figured out? Were you totally un-messy? Of course not! Take time to celebrate those moments and acknowledge how far you've already come.

2

FAILURE
DON'T STICK THE LANDING

• • •

Failure is not an option—it is mandatory. The option is whether or not to let failure be the last thing you do.

HOWARD TAYLER, writer and illustrator

THE AUTHENTICITY MAP

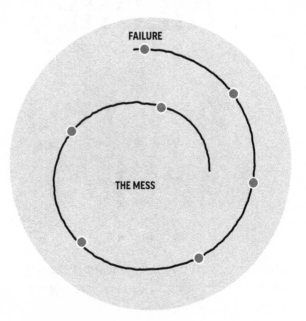

N THE summer of 1984, I was seven years old. I grew up on a dirt road in a tiny rural town, the second of fifteen children. We weren't usually allowed to hang out in the house in the summertime. When the weather was good, my mom would shoo us all out the door in the morning, and we'd run wild until the fireflies came out. I'm pretty sure that our being out of the house from dawn to dusk was her favorite part of summer.

But for two weeks in August 1984, my mom made an exception, and I spent the evenings in front of our little television set, totally enthralled—because that year, Mary Lou Retton was on TV.

She was sixteen years old, and in 1984 she would become the first American female to win an individual all-round gold medal in Olympic gymnastics. Overall, she took home five medals that year. (Can I just pause to repeat that she was freaking *sixteen* years old?!)

Mary Lou was a superhero to girls all over the world. She is the reason I begged my dad to build me a balance beam that summer. She was the first female athlete to be pictured on a Wheaties box. (Let's be honest, she was probably the only reason why most of us ate Wheaties at all.)

As I grew older, I realized that we only saw a small portion of her journey. In an interview later in life, Mary Lou said, "Back in my era, gymnasts were pixies, slender, very graceful little butterflies... I wasn't. I wasn't a pretty, little gymnast. I was a very powerful, explosive gymnast."

She added, "When people see us standing on the podium with medals draped around our neck, that's just the pinnacle of our success. But all of us have a story of struggle, a story of overcoming adversity to actually get here."

Mary Lou didn't fit the mold of what success looked like. In fact, she wasn't expected to succeed that year at all. Just five weeks prior to the Olympics, she'd undergone knee surgery and was still recovering.

That was the summer when I first learned the term "stick the landing." This means to finish an athletic, gymnastic, or other sports performance with an ideal pose or stance, especially after a jump or leap.

If we apply this to life in the way that most people do, it means that how we finish is all that matters. That no matter what happens in the messy middle, we have to make it look good when we are on the mat. But I think this is the exact kind of mindset that screws us up so badly and keeps us from moving forward toward authenticity and joy.

I am going to tell you something that you probably don't know about Olympic gymnastics. Something that might initially make you angry... I know it pissed me right off when I first learned about it.

When a gymnast lands a tumbling pass, a vault, or a dismount, and plants their feet, it is called a stuck landing. On floor exercise, men are expected to stick their tumbling passes, while women are allowed to take one step back without deduction.

Let me repeat that: *women are allowed to take a step back—without deduction.* These are the official rules of Olympic gymnastics. Holy moly, that pissed me off. What the heck? Are women considered weaker? They think we can't stick the landing, and men can? Women get a pass? Why?

But the more I thought about this rule, the more I realized that this is exactly what we should be doing. All of us. Taking a step back and learning from the process that got us there. Taking a step back and gathering ourselves for the next move. We should all feel free to do that.

When we accept that we are allowed to do that, without deduction, think of the possibilities that might open up for us! Think of how freeing it is to know that we don't have to stay stuck in failure!

Stumbles, struggles, failures… call them whatever you like, the reality is that we all have them. They are not always epic or public, but they happen to us all.

Many of us are so focused on sticking the landing, looking good on the podium, and living up to everyone's expectations that a single failure can send us into a dark hole.

As leaders, we are often so afraid of what others will say about our missteps that we disregard the learning and leading opportunities that come with our struggles.

The first step out of failure and toward authenticity is admitting that everyone fails. Failure happens to everyone. It's inevitable. In fact, it's a critical part of growth and learning. The key is to keep going after the failure.

• • •

GOOD GRIEF

Talking about failure is tricky. It can feel like something terrible that we did, instead of something that is part of being human. When my life fell apart, I crawled into a hole, pitched a tent, and forwarded my mail there. I kept trying to figure out what I had done wrong... what I could have done differently. It never occurred to me that this was not only a normal part of growth and life, it was also a necessary part of becoming the person I was meant to be.

When I was trying to get perspective on the idea of failure and longing for more joy in my life and work, I reached out to Shabnam Mogharabi, the former CEO and co-founder of SoulPancake. Shabnam is a self-described purveyor of joy and cultivator of hope, on a mission to tell stories that lift people up, and she does this in profound and beautiful ways.

But I asked her: What about failure? The dark hole that many of us start in? What is your advice for us? How do we crawl out of that hole toward joy and hope? Where do we start?

Her response was breathtakingly truthful.

"First you have to address the grief because a lot of the negative feelings around failure are really grief," she said. "And grief is a funny one. If you've ever lost someone in your life, you know that grief is a very strange emotion. It doesn't hit you all at once. You can sometimes be numb to it, and then eventually it'll come back, or someone will say something, or you'll smell something, and it'll remind you of that person. And all of a sudden you have that wave of grief again.

"I think oftentimes people look at failure and they think, *Oh, it means something's broken in me.* But what's actually happening when you feel failure is you're feeling grief over this thing that didn't succeed, or this door that didn't open, or this opportunity that didn't happen, or this business that failed. And there's a lot of grief around that. And grief has to be dealt with in a different way. Grief has to be allowed to unfold over time."

"OMG," I said, "you are so right! Grief isn't a quick fix. It's a long-term emotion that comes and goes. I wasn't a failure for sobbing in that closet! I was grieving, and trying to handle it like there was a simple solution."

Shabnam replied, "The term 'failure' has such negative connotations. But if we reframe failure as grief over the lost opportunity or the thing that didn't manifest that we were so hoping for, I think it's easier for us to manage and wrap our heads around. We can say, 'Oh yes, I recognize this. I understand what grief is. I know grief takes time to heal.' I think it becomes a lot easier to deal with when you reframe failure as grief."

She went on, "I also believe that failure is sometimes just a door closing because there's another door out there that needs to open for you. And it may not open tomorrow. It may not open for five years or ten years, but it just means that there was a force at play that meant that wasn't for you. It is not a reflection of who you are. Maybe it just wasn't right at the right time. So, I do think we need to reframe the way we think about failure. I think it's actually more grief that we're dealing with."

Long after our conversation, I kept coming back to the same question: What if we reframed failure as grief at work? How would that change our perspective?

We tend to have a low tolerance for failure at work. All the metrics, KPIs, and goalposts measure productivity, output, and success. Failure is not universally expected or accepted. But what about grief?

. . .

> "Grief has to be dealt with
>
> in a different way. Grief has to be
>
> allowed to unfold over time."

. . .

When someone is grieving, we understand that. We feel sympathy. We gather around them and support them. This is an emotion we can all understand and respond to.

A few years after her husband's tragic death, Sheryl Sandberg wrote *Option B*, a book in which she chronicled her own journey from grief to joy. In it, she shared the work of Martin Seligman, a psychologist who has spent decades studying how people deal with failure and the grief that follows.

Seligman found that when things go wrong, we often default to the three P's. First, personalization: *This is my fault. I suck.* Second, pervasiveness: *Everything sucks.* And third, permanence: *It's always going to suck.*

When I read that, I realized that, like most humans, I am guilty of going down that road far too often. And the truth is, not only is that not helpful, it's simply not true.

The more I thought about this—the idea of reframing failure as grief, and the trap of the three P's—the more I realized that this is where I was that day in the utility closet. My life had catastrophically imploded and I was deeply grieving. But I was also convinced that I sucked, everything sucked, and it always would suck.

There is no quick fix for grief. And failure is inevitable. Both are normal, human experiences. And yet so many of us get stuck in this place on the map. Like me, you may have pitched a tent and forwarded your mail. I know people who have hung out in this space for years, never taking that first step forward.

This starting point is so critical to authenticity. We simply cannot lead others if we are stuck in the mindset that failure and messiness mean that we suck, everything sucks, and it will always suck.

Building on Seligman's concept, I have learned to replace those three P's with new words. Now, when I experience failure and grief and I am tempted to wallow in the suckiness of all the things, instead I remind myself I can change my perspective through three simple words.

Protection: *this is keeping me from something not meant for me.*
This step is so critical, but it can be super hard to acknowledge in the moment. We stamp our feet and say, "But I wanted that! That opportunity or path or job or relationship or promotion would have been so great for me! How can anything else be better?" But we can't see the future, and we don't know who we are going to need to be to

handle what is ahead. This protection may be exactly what we need to become that person.

Possibility: *when things go wrong, everything else is possible.* This single word can change so much. When change happens, when failure happens, when a crisis happens... possibility also happens. A door has closed. You now know what is not going to work. That means everything else is possible. Literally every other option becomes a possibility.

Permission: *now I can try something else.*
So you failed. Guess what? Life just wrote you a big, fat permission slip to try something else. What a gift! Take it and run with it!

I am still going to fail and grieve—we all are. But now we can also accept that being a messy leader, an authentic leader, means that along with failure comes possibility and permission.

. . .

FAILING LIKE A BOSS

As a young manager, hiring was one of my biggest challenges. I made some bad calls, but none so bad as when I hired Denise (not her real name). Denise was one of those people who interviewed really well. She knew all the right things to say and all the right names to drop. She was witty and bright. I was convinced she was the perfect candidate. And on her first day on the job, I knew I'd made a terrible mistake.

As an interviewee, she was pleasant and bubbly. As an employee, she was pessimistic, critical, and negative. There wasn't a situation or a person that she couldn't find fault with. Every request or project was met with resistance and questioning. I noticed an immediate shift in the culture of my team, and it wasn't positive.

I remember going to my boss at the end of the first week and saying, "I need to fire Denise." My boss blinked at me like I'd lost my mind. Yes, it had been only a week. Yes, we'd just completed many weeks of interviewing and juggling. Yes, this was an inconvenient and, frankly, embarrassing thing that I was admitting. But it was the truth. And it felt like a failure.

That wasn't the first or the last time I made a mistake as a leader. But over time, I learned some very important lessons about failure.

First, I learned to fail not *on* purpose, but *with* purpose. No leader ever wants to fail on purpose. We don't set out to fail. (Hey, let's see if this can end spectacularly badly with my team in chaos and me eating my feelings!) But it happens. It's inevitable. However, if we can learn to fail *with* purpose, now we're getting somewhere.

Failing with purpose means that every time something doesn't work, you learn something new, make the right changes, and then try again (and possibly fail again), faster and faster each time.

In 2019, scientists at Northwestern University published a study on failure. They based their study on an analysis of 776,721 grant applications submitted to the National Institutes of Health over thirty years, as well as forty-six years' worth of venture capital start-up investments, and less conventionally, 170,350 terrorist attacks carried out over a nearly fifty-year span.

The biggest takeaway from their study was that every success starts with a failure. Their research showed that what ultimately separates those who succeed from those who fail is not persistence, but iterations.

The old adage—"try, try again"—as it turns out, only works if you learn from your failures.

Dashun Wang, the scientist who headed the study, said, "You have to figure out what worked and what didn't, and then focus on what needs to be improved instead of thrashing around and changing everything. The people who failed didn't necessarily work less. They could actually have worked more; it's just that they made more unnecessary changes."

Wang's team found that a key predictor of success is the time between consecutive failed attempts, which should decrease progressively. In other words, the faster you fail, the better your chances of success, and the more time that goes by between attempts, the more likely you are to fail again. They went so far as to call failure "an essential prerequisite" for success.

The second thing I learned was to *always fail forward*. Failure is, by nature, a roadblock. It can stop us from moving forward if we let it. There's a reason it is the first stop on the map. Many people spend their entire careers in that void, never getting to joy and authenticity.

But when we fail forward, we learn to use each failure to propel us toward the next step. It can create momentum if we let it. Hiring and then firing Denise felt like a failure.

I could have easily internalized that failure and sat with it, letting it pull me backward into doubt and resistance. But instead it created momentum for me and my team. I learned to include more diverse roles and voices in the hiring process, put in place some new interview practices, and, ultimately, hire more slowly and fire faster in the future.

The third thing I learned is that *failure is not the worst thing that can happen*. The worst thing is letting failure stop us from learning and moving forward. The worst thing is living in a perpetual state of *I suck, everything sucks, it's always going to suck*.

• • •

The old adage—"try, try again"—

as it turns out, only works

if you learn from your failures.

• • •

In general, I think we have a pretty negative view of failures. Just the word itself gives me the ick. (Like "winners" and "losers." Ugh. I hate those words.) Reframing failure as grief or disappointment is helpful, but we have to also remind ourselves that we need failures to learn and grow and improve—those lessons are important. Imagine where we would be if we never experienced failures or setbacks? I find it hard to believe that we wouldn't all be insufferable douchebags if we never failed at anything.

Learning to learn from failure is a practice. It requires intentional post-mortems after every failure and every success. Teams that implement this practice are stronger, more resilient, and recover faster from setbacks. When we make failures an expected part of the process, an inevitable part of growth, that is when the magic happens.

As a leader, this realization meant that I went from dreading failure to celebrating it. I know what you're thinking: *Celebrating failure? Have you lost your mind?* But seriously, when things go wrong, celebrating means we immediately switch to the three P's: *Cool. That didn't work. Now everything else is possible and I can try something new.*

Perhaps the most important lesson I have learned about failure was the toughest: Don't cling to mistakes because you spent a long time making them. Geez Louise, this one was tough. I can think of so many times I have made things so much worse for myself and my team because I hung on to mistakes until my hands bled. It's so tempting to think, *Well, we've come this far and sunk this many resources into this, we probably shouldn't just scrap it and walk away.* But the truth is, starting over is often quicker and far less costly.

As leaders, we often think that we have to see something through because of how much time and money we've invested. The psychologist, Elliot Aronson studied this back in the 1950s. He got a group of people and put them in a very boring book club. Everyone there was purposely, intentionally dull. He then asked them to rate how good the club was. Next, he got another group of people and made them go through a rigorous testing process to get into the same book club.

The people who had done the rigorous testing—completed surveys and applications to get into the book club, even though it was super boring—reported that the book club was amazing. Their scores were far and away better than the people who didn't have to do anything to get in. This speaks to the psychological bias that we often have as leaders—we trick ourselves into believing that something is good because of the sunk costs.

Learning to fail faster, more intentionally, and with purpose didn't happen overnight. It took years of practice, and I have much more of it ahead of me. But these lessons continue to guide me every time I screw up. Remembering them and applying them keep me from getting stuck in the darkest part of the map, and ensure that I continue to be an authentic leader, even when times are messy.

• • •

STUMBLE, RECOVER, FOLLOW THROUGH

Years ago, I heard Alison Levine speak at an event. Alison is a mountain climber who has ascended the highest peaks on every continent and skied to both the North and South Poles. Her résumé is hella impressive—an internship at Mattel, a stint at Goldman Sachs, and then deputy finance director for Arnold Schwarzenegger, then governor of California. She's even served as an adjunct professor for the United States Military Academy.

But the part that stood out to me was when she told the story of how her team, the first American Women's Everest Expedition, turned back a few hundred feet short of Everest's summit in May 2002.

Can you imagine? All that training, all that preparation, all that time... and then to have to turn back when the summit is so close you can almost taste it? Some would call that a colossal failure. But not Levine. "Backing up," she said in her talk, "is not the same as backing down."

What a freeing thing to hear!

There are times in life when we learn that we have to let go. We hate those times because it often feels like we're giving up. But backing up isn't the same as backing down. It's okay to take a step back, to care for yourself, to adjust, to take a new path. It's not the same as giving up. It's not a failure. It's part of the process.

In July 2021, Simone Biles, one of the greatest athletes of our time, withdrew from the team competition at the Olympics. Citing her mental health concerns, she stepped back, cheered on her team, and chose not to compete in an event she had trained for her entire life.

Soon after, I saw that a friend had posted on Facebook that "GOATs don't quit." It took my breath away.

At the same time Simone Biles was backing up, I was struggling with depression. I worked, smiled, laughed, traveled, got on stage, ran a business, and pretended everything was fine. But I was not fine.

A week before Simone made that excruciating decision, I hit a wall. I came very close to taking my own life. I found myself on the floor, crying, telling my mom that I couldn't do any of it anymore. It was the scariest moment of my life.

Thankfully, with the support of some dear friends, I went to see a doctor, and I got help. I sat in that doctor's office and wept as I told her that taking medicine and getting help felt like I was failing. It felt like admitting that because I couldn't just struggle through, I was somehow giving up.

That doctor stood up, put her hands on either side of my face, and said, "Getting help is not failing. It's not giving up. It's the *right thing.*"

Statistically, most of us are struggling. We are all dealing with work and grief and life and finances and kids and parents and pandemics. Getting help is not quitting. Pausing to set boundaries and care for yourself is not failing. Saying no is not failing. Backing up is not the same as backing down.

No matter how long you worked for something, no matter your status or title, no matter your occupation, no matter if you are standing at the freaking Olympics... getting help is not failing or quitting. And if it is, then the *real* GOATs quit all the damn time.

I think back to that summer of 1984 and Mary Lou Retton and the term "stick the landing."

Just like Mary Lou, many of us don't fit the mold of what success looks like. Many of us stand on the podium and know that no one really understands the struggle it took to get there. Instead of the Olympics, our podium may look like a boardroom table, a Zoom call, or a year-end awards ceremony. Maybe others don't expect us to succeed. Maybe we've also had to take a step back.

As leaders, we aren't just allowed to take a step back and learn from the process that got us there—it's critical that we do. We should all be taking a step back and gathering ourselves for the next move, *without deduction*. We should be reminding those who work with us that they also need to prioritize the process over appearing perfect for everyone watching.

Whatever the truth is for gymnastics is the same truth no matter what business you are in. It's not really about sticking the landing. It's about allowing yourself and others the ability to stumble, recover, and keep going.

If we truly want to become joyful, authentic (and messy) leaders, we have to start by unlearning that failure is the end point. In reality, it's only the beginning.

SELF-ASSESSMENT
• • •

What Do You Need to Unlearn?
- What is your default response when you experience a failure at work?
- Do you have a process in place that allows you to identify learnings from failures?
- In what areas of your life do you need to allow yourself to step back without deduction?

Get Started
What is your failure pattern? Think about your go-to process when things go sideways. Where does your mindset take you? In order to move forward on the map, first you must admit that failure is inevitable and also immensely useful in the process. Putting an intentional post-mortem system in place will help you to move more quickly from failure into protection, possibility, and permission. Think of the last time you dealt with a mistake or disappointment. What did it protect you from? What did it make possible? And what did it give you permission to do next? How can you apply that mindset in the future?

CELEBRATE!

How can you start to celebrate the possibilities rather than wallow in the missteps? You've tried something and it hasn't worked. Great. Now everything else is a possibility! Start a failure celebration habit with your team. This might feel counter-productive at first, but celebrating what didn't work can be just as powerful as celebrating what did. Remember, as Howard Tayler said, "Failure is not an option—it is mandatory. The option is whether or not to let failure be the last thing you do."

DENIAL

● ● ●

Life is like the monkey bars:
you have to let go to move forward.
LEAH BUSQUE, founder of TaskRabbit

'VE BEEN known to get stuck in a rut of self-doubt. I stand in my rubber boots in a big giant puddle of Poor Me. I'm not embarrassed to admit it, because we all wallow in that puddle sometimes. But sometimes I really dig in.

I called my mom once to tell her about my puddle. I spent a lot of time explaining all the reasons I should be miserable. I made a list. It was extensive. She listened. She told me she loved me. And then she said, "How deep is this puddle? Is it up over your boots? Is it up to your armpits? Can you move your arms and legs? Can you breathe?"

Sigh. "Yes, Mom. I can move and breathe."

"Good," she said, "then move."

Move. It seems so obvious. So simple. Just start doing something other than standing still, staring at the puddle. I don't know if there's a single other boot-wearing, puddle-wallowing person out there but if there is ... it's time to move.

We can wallow in our failures, our disappointments, and our grief for only so long. At some point, if we want things to change, we have to move.

There are a whole lot of people who never get past the failure stage. They spend their lives, their careers, and their relationships sitting in that puddle, staring at it. The first step forward is to admit we can't do everything, we aren't always going to succeed at everything, and failure is a starting point.

You might be thinking, *Nope. Not me. This isn't about me. I'm not stuck in failure. I'm fine.* But the reality is that most of us start out here. And if we never admit it, we never move past it.

If we can achieve true authenticity as leaders, if we can show up as our whole, human selves, still messy but moving from *I suck, everything sucks, it's always going to suck* to *Everything is possible,* think of the work we could do and the people we could serve! And think of what a relief it would be to not have to pretend!

This was the turning point for me that day in the utility closet. The point where I stopped pretending that everything was sunshine and roses, and I started telling the truth about my job and my life.

I won't lie—this wasn't an overnight process. I started that day by being honest with my boss. We sat in that utility closet, and I told her why I couldn't keep standing on stages and pretending everything was fine. Just letting someone in was a huge relief. Being honest was like flipping on a light in a very dark hallway.

I stopped pretending and started telling people that I was messy. That everything isn't always easy or perfect or Instagrammable. Instead of closing myself off from all the emotions, and leaving them at the door, I started using them as my superpower. They made me a more empathetic, more compassionate, and more joyful leader.

The first step is moving past denial. And some of you reading this may not even realize that you are in denial. You probably think that this is just what work is meant to feel like—a slog. A daily grind to survive or get through.

But there might be a part of you that is wondering, *Is there more out there? Is there more to the work that I'm doing? Is this it?*

The good news: the answer is yes. There is more out there. There is more to the work that you're doing. You don't have to stay stuck in this place on the map. You can overcome this roadblock.

You simply have to decide that you want to continue moving toward joy.

3

FEAR
DO IT
SCARED

● ● ●

*Remember that the minute you take the first
step into the life of your dreams, the first to
greet you there will be fear. Nod. Keep walking.*

BRIANNA WIEST, *The Mountain Is You:
Transforming Self-Sabotage into Self-Mastery*

THE AUTHENTICITY MAP

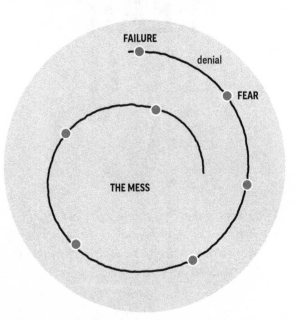

FAILURE

denial

FEAR

THE MESS

YEARS AGO, I worked for a real estate firm that was always looking for creative ways to improve employee morale. We worked long hours in a competitive market with high-stakes, luxury clients. A small mistake could have big consequences.

To reward us for a job done well, the boss implemented an employee of the month program. Each month, a person was chosen who embodied the values of the brand and produced exemplary work.

If you were named the employee of the month, the reward was a true experience—something that would push you outside your comfort zone or bring you joy. Some employees were given weekends away in wine country, with horseback rides on the beach. Another received the experience of tandem skydiving. Yet another got a ride in a hot air balloon. We celebrated our wins, and we celebrated each other.

Finally, it was my turn. It was exciting just to receive the honor. We all worked hard to achieve the title—the experience was just the icing on the figurative cake. I remember opening the envelope in anticipation and seeing two words at the top of the page: *Shark Dive*.

Did I mention I was living in Australia at the time?

Don't worry. My boss didn't load me into a cage and drop me into open waters churning with great whites. But he may as well have. I'd lived in Australia for a few years at that point, but I'd never been scuba diving. Truth be told, I think I was more frightened of the diving part than the shark part.

The day came for me to dive, and I was a nervous wreck. I was diving in the (now closed) Manly Sea Life Sanctuary, a four-million-liter oceanarium, home to several species of sharks, stingrays, and sea turtles. The adventure started with a basic scuba lesson and a few warnings about what not to do (no sudden movements, don't swim upwards without checking that there are no sharks above you—you know... the important stuff), and then came the instruction to duck my head and dive through the door into the open water.

But right before I did that, my guide turned to me and said, "Oh, and one more thing: if the power goes out and it gets dark, don't panic. Have fun!"

Wait. What?

At that exact moment, it occurred to me that I was diving into open water, lit by electrical lights that, if they went out, would leave me in utter darkness, surrounded by sharks, breathing through a tube.

Have fun?!

A hundred scenarios raced through my head as I placed the regulator in my mouth, took a breath, and dove.

I remember a few things about that dive. I remember the sharks gliding past like silent, silver, toothy vampires. I remember the stingrays, the size of double mattresses, swooshing up against me. I remember the sound of my quickened breath coming in and out, and my guide handing me a shark tooth he'd found on the ocean floor, gesturing for me to tuck it in the sleeve of my wetsuit. But mostly, I remember the fact that the entire time I was afraid.

Fear is a funny emotion. We all get scared, but we all have vastly different limits for what makes us feel fear. Some of us love horror movies and haunted houses, while others (me) will cover our eyes when things get even a little tense on *Grey's Anatomy*.

Fear is also an important point on The Authenticity Map—because it's a point where we have to make a decision.

No matter what makes you feel fear, thanks to the amygdala, your body reacts the same as everyone else's—your heart rate increases, your breath becomes shallow, your skin prickles, and your stomach flip-flops. The amygdala is our brain's security alarm, and without it, humans probably would not have survived much past the Bronze Age.

When bad news comes in the form of sight, sound, taste, touch, or pain, the amygdala sends a signal for the body to respond by increasing our heart rate, blood pressure, and respiration. A surge of adrenaline, a stress hormone, is pumped into our bloodstream, which triggers the fight-or-flight instinct. We freeze while our bodies and brains assess the danger and decide whether we should stand our ground or run away—and all of this happens within fractions of a second.

Whether you love horror films or not, this isn't a fun process for our bodies. We can't physically operate for long periods with elevated heart rates and immense amounts of stress hormones pulsing through our veins. Our organs would eventually shut down from the stress. The fact is, the state of fear isn't a fun or practical place to live long term.

We often stay in a place of grief and failure at work because it can feel like one of those Snuggies you see on late-night infomercials. It can feel cozy and safe to stay miserable and in denial. It's the devil we know, after all. And knowing that the first step out of that numbness is fear— well, that isn't exactly a motivational thought. (Leave your failure behind! Next stop, fear! How fun!)

And yet, if we are doing our job right, we are bumping up against failures regularly. To move past them, sometimes we just have to take a deep breath and dive into the shark tank.

I remember a friend telling me once how she had learned to swim. On a family beach vacation, she'd spent days standing on the dock in her pink arm floaties, watching her family in the water, hearing them coax her to jump in. Finally, one day, she told her mother to just push her, because she was never going to do it otherwise.

We can't control the fear reaction in our bodies. The amygdala is gonna amygdala, no matter what. But we can learn to do it scared. In fact, we must, because the alternative is never advancing through the mess. I could have skipped the shark dive. I could have decided it was too scary. But by doing it scared, I learned that I was capable of doing incredible things, even when my entire brain was screaming at me to stop. And to be honest, to this day, it is one of my favorite memories. I look back and think, *I did that thing that so many others wouldn't have done, and it made me braver and stronger and more daring.*

• • •

SPIDEY SENSES

My friend Brad Montague, a *New York Times* bestselling author and co-creator of the web series *Kid President*, describes fear as "a sign of being in the zip code of something interesting."

The way Spiderman has his spidey sense, fear appears for him as "Oh, something is about to happen"—like an opportunity to grow or face something. Brad says that the presence of fear or the looming approach of it can help point you toward what you care about.

When I got to this part of The Authenticity Map, I knew that I needed to talk to Brad. He's never sugarcoated fear—or emotions of any kind—in all the years I have known him. So I called him up and asked him how he handles fear.

"You are amazing," I said. "Look at all the crazy cool, interesting, creative projects you've done! But do you ever get scared? I mean, of course you do. So, how do you handle it?"

Brad describes "the fog of fear" as something we must navigate. A place on the map that we shouldn't totally avoid, but approach with caution. "Fear is a little companion there on my shoulder, letting me know that there's a version of this in which I don't show up well," he says. "What I'd like to do is to show up as my best self and be as present as I can in every moment. What fear wants to do is distract us from that. But if our antennae are in the right place, fear can also become a signal letting us know 'Hey, you might want to be present for this. You need to be fully here.'"

The brilliant writer and artist Meera Lee Patel refers to fear as her friend. "Fear is a friend and it's here to support you," she writes in her book, *My Friend Fear*. "Like all friendships, the one you have with fear is a two-way street. It requires us to sit with it, listen to it, and try our best to understand it—even though we don't always know how. Like any friend, fear can only help you if you let it. Fear is always beside us, but it doesn't keep us from freedom: it leads us to it, slowly moving us toward the magic."

I like the idea of fear being a loving Jiminy Cricket on your shoulder or a friend who wants to help you. That makes it so much less... well, scary.

But sometimes it is scary.

At work, we can typically divide fearful moments into two camps. There are moments when fear is holding us back from doing something brave and good or risky and necessary—these moments can motivate us. And there are moments when fear is keeping us safe from real hazards— we have to learn to navigate these moments safely.

Years ago, I sat in the audience with several thousand others, listening to a gifted speaker. He had just finished a rousing, inspiring talk. He'd shared ways that companies large and small had done amazing, creative, and risky things. He had encouraged us to do the same. And then he asked if there were any questions.

There was a hush over the crowd, and then a few hands went up.

"What if it doesn't work?"

"But what happens if it fails?"

"But how does that work for me?"

"What if I do it wrong?"

Question after question, the audience had immediately started worrying about failure instead of success—before even making a single attempt.

This kind of fear is natural and normal. As a leader of a team, you'll bump up against this often. But if you allow it to paralyze you and stop you from trying new things, that is when it becomes a problem.

Jon Acuff describes this so well. He says, "Fear is a wonderful teacher but a terrible CEO. If you ignore its lessons, you'll never know which dragons need to be slayed. If you ask it to be the boss, it will keep your life small because all it can see are dragons. Learn from fear but don't let it lead."

Recognizing when fear is simply trying to keep you from discomfort is key. In these situations, we have to teach our brains to choose fight over flight.

Public speaking is a great example. It's no shark dive, of course, but it's estimated that 75 percent of adults have some level of anxiety about speaking in front of a crowd. And yet studies show that those who either master this skill or speak despite their anxiety are more likely to be promoted and achieve a higher income.

When I first started public speaking, it felt a bit like walking in waist-deep water. I was making progress, but it felt like I was pushing against a wall of resistance. My amygdala was flashing warning signs at me that I was doing something that felt unsafe. But over time, I learned that I could override that alarm. Sure, I still get nervous, but no longer does my brain tell me that I am in danger when I step on a stage. I never would have gotten to that place if I hadn't started doing it scared.

But what about the times when our amygdala is right?

The first month on the job in my first corporate role, I attended a leadership retreat. At the end of the day, when the meetings were finished, I got into the elevator with a married, older male co-worker, and once the doors closed, he turned to me, a married, twenty-something woman and said, "Your room or mine?" To him, it was a throwaway joke. To me, it felt threatening.

Later, in another role, I worked with a male COO who would regularly come into my office, close the door, and threaten and berate me while standing with his back against the door, blocking my only exit. It left me keenly aware that every office I ever had was designed to face the door, leaving me with no escape whenever this happened.

I had a senior colleague who once told me not to "worry my pretty little head" about a policy that I objected to, in front of the entire leadership team, and no one said a word.

More times than I can count I have had male bosses and managers make lewd jokes in my presence, expect that I'd look the other way from their drunken behavior at holiday parties, and suggest that what happens at conferences doesn't count.

This is, unfortunately, a regular workplace occurrence for many women, especially women of color, and LGBTQ+ people. This is not the kind of fear we should be embracing. These are the moments when our amygdala is right. These are not safe environments. Unhealthy fear is never acceptable in a workplace. Tell someone. Document. Seek help. Don't be silent. Fear that tells us we are unsafe and in unhealthy environments is fear that should be paid careful attention to. In these cases, our spidey senses are usually correct.

But the fear that holds us back from productive momentum, taking good risks, and trying new things (even though we may fail) is fear that we can face and overcome. This is the fear that we can make our friend. This is the fear that will help us move forward toward authenticity.

• • •

SET SAIL

Any addict will tell you that the first step in recovery is admitting you have a problem. This is the first step toward navigating fear in your career as well: admitting you are scared. However, this tends to go against some of the most ingrained lies we tell ourselves at work. As I've already talked about, the idea that we are supposed to "fake it 'til we make it" or "never let them see you sweat" is outdated and unrealistic.

It's totally normal to feel scared of moving outside your comfort zone! There is no such thing as a fearless leader. The good news is, there is a way to move through fear and ultimately past it.

First, admit it. Acknowledge your fear and tell the truth about it. The best result I ever had with my team was when I admitted I was also out of my comfort zone. It gave everyone the space to take a deep breath and admit the same.

Brad Montague told me a story about a time in college when he had the chance to meet one of his musical heroes, Jonathan Michael Richman, founder of the Modern Lovers, an influential proto-punk band.

"He was a punk rock guy, but he also sang about ice cream trucks," Brad said. "He had this storied career doing all sorts of really weird but cool music. And then he moved into singing really simple songs, and I was drawn to those childlike songs. I was so excited to meet him. He is a legend and I wanted to ask him, 'Hey, I'm this college student and I'm an artist. How do I make it as an artist?' I caught him as he was packing up cords after a show, and I wanted him to give me advice. Instead he just like looked at me and went, 'Just tell the truth, man.'"

Brad laughed as he got to this part of the story. "That's all he said. And I felt like, *What does that even mean? What is he talking about?* But the more I thought about it, I realized in my favorite songs of his, that's literally all he did. That's all punk rock was in the early days. They just would simplify it down to a few chords and a few lines that said exactly what they wanted to say. And that's what made his music so simple. It comes down to the economy of words. *Just tell the truth, man.* I realized how much I love that, and I'm grateful when people can so beautifully convey the truth. And yet I was avoiding that because I wanted to impress others or do things for approval or applause. But true connection happens with candor and with honesty."

Just tell the truth. A simple but effective first step toward navigating fear.

Next, own it. It's easy to blame others for doing or saying things that scare you, but no one can make you scared. That's your own amygdala, baby. One simple change in your perspective can be powerful—instead of saying "I'm scared," try saying "I have fear about this." This feeling doesn't define who you are. It's simply a normal chemical reaction in your brain, one that you can move past.

Finally, do something. Take bold and brave steps, even if your nerves are tagging along. Your legs and voice may shake, but move forward. Don't hold back from embracing risks, making those asks, testing out new waters, or making a move.

Fear has its moments—it can slam the brakes on being authentic, expressing our truths, and chasing after what we are meant to do. But if we remind ourselves that it's just our amygdala trying to save us from a saber-toothed tiger, and we're ready to face those fears with openness and guts, magic happens.

What would you do if you weren't afraid? *Screw that.* What is possible if you have fear but do it anyway?

Even when you do this—admit your fear, own it, and take action, things may still not work out. Things will go wrong. Mistakes will be made. Lessons will be learned. You may even find yourself tempted to slide back into the dark hole of failure. (Fear would love that! Its entire goal is to get us to run away!)

Brad Montague likens this process to being a ship-wrecked sailor. As a discouraged sailor, the first thing you do is steady your boat. Maybe it has to be rebuilt or maybe there's been some critical damage, but steady the boat first. Then look at your compass. Before you get in the water again, before you set sail, identify that thing you cared about that got you started in the first place or the destination you want to reach. Then find the wind and set sail.

"But," he adds, "a final step I've added is to invite ship-mates. Find some other people to help you address what fell apart the last time or just to go on the journey with you."

That really is the definition of leadership after all, isn't it? It's the role of a leader to steady the boat, consult the compass, and find the wind. But the very best leaders bring others along with them.

My very first real mentor at work was a man named Tom Kuiper. He was a great leader who told me a secret that has stayed with me for decades. I asked him once why the salespeople in the office were often so mean or tense. He said, "They all walk around scared all the time." It surprised me because these were grown adults who earned big paychecks and had achieved great success.

$\bullet \ \bullet \ \bullet$

What would you do if you weren't
afraid? *Screw that*. What is possible
if you have fear but do it anyway?

$\bullet \ \bullet \ \bullet$

Over time, however, I realized the truth of what he had said. We all walk around with fear. We are scared of doing something wrong, scared of losing a deal, scared of losing a paycheck, scared of losing a friend, or scared of missing an opportunity. We are afraid to fail out loud or stand out too much. We are afraid to not be vanilla enough or to be the extra scoop of full-fat chunky monkey that we already are. We are constantly in a state of fear.

Learning that secret gave me empathy and made me a better leader and teacher. But there is a second part to that secret that I learned much later.

As Marianne Williamson said, "Our deepest fear is not that we are inadequate. Our deepest fear is that we are powerful beyond measure." Our biggest fear is that we are awesome, freaking superstars.

Because if we are superstars, that means we have the power and the responsibility to do something with all of that awesome. If we admit that we are badass, then we know that we are meant to do something with it. Because playing small does not serve the world.

I believe that we are all created to do big things. But first, we have to believe that we can, and then we have to be brave enough to do something about it. Leadership coach Kristin Lohr, of We Are Soul Sparks, says, "You must become unshakeable in the belief that you are worthy of a big life." We don't just have the power to be awesome; we are worthy of a big, bold, badass life. And we all need to believe that.

I love Brad's analogy about leadership and shipwrecks. But the best—and most important—part of the story is the last part. The part where we are reminded to bring people with us.

Leadership is messy. It's messy because it's not just about you. It's also about the people you bring along with you. And because those people are human, they come with a whole menu of complicated emotions, backstories, and hang-ups.

There are plenty of times when it would just be easier to focus on ourselves. Go it alone, when stuff is hard and going wrong. When it doesn't just rain—it pours. Our team is struggling. We've hired the wrong people, or our systems aren't working. Our business is struggling. Our relationship is a hot mess. Our bills are unpaid. When that happens, for many of us, our instinct is to circle the wagons, board up the windows, and keep it all to ourselves.

Using Brad's analogy, it might just be easier to set sail alone.

As leaders, it's tempting to hunker down and only emerge from that season of our lives when the worst is over. When the pain has mostly passed, we can see the finish line, the scab is healing, and the resolution is in sight. Then we are triumphant and ready to show up again.

But real leadership happens in the messy middle. Something powerful and important happens in the part when the end is not in sight and the resolution is not guaranteed. When all you can do is the next right thing. There is something in that moment—in the messy, dirty, real, painful, struggling middle—that is getting you to the finish line. That is the real story. And while that can be scary to talk about or live out loud with our people, this is where authentic leadership really happens—in the mess.

● ● ●

DISTURB THE UNIVERSE

So, how do we lead ourselves and our team out of fear and toward joy? We know the amygdala is coming along for the ride, but there has to be a way out, right?

I asked Brad this question. He's written bestselling books, made a television show for the Magnolia Network, co-created a viral web series, and produced amazing art that has impacted countless people. But he's also had projects fail and pitches that didn't go anywhere. How did he crack the code of moving beyond failure and fear?

"There's this thing people say to encourage themselves," he said. *"Nobody knows what they're doing."*

He went on, "I've told myself that before too, especially working in television or in media, and seeing that a lot of the people who make these decisions or do these things that I'm afraid of also don't always know what they're doing. And when I feel like I'm just a kid from a small town in Tennessee at the grownups' table, saying, 'I don't belong in this room,' I've also told myself they don't know what they're doing either.

• • •

Real leadership happens

in the messy middle.

• • •

"But I have learned to flip that from 'nobody knows what they're doing' to 'everybody knows something.' And that includes me. So even in those rooms where I feel like I don't belong, or those spaces where I feel like maybe I'm afraid to show up, I recognize that everyone in the room has something that I can learn from and I have something I can contribute too."

Brad adds, "In recent years, I have realized how important it is to speak up and raise the flag when I think I'm in over my head. It's not just unfounded fear; I'm recognizing that I need some assistance. That has caused me to get out of my comfort zone and express some vulnerability and bring in help on projects or just bring on ears to listen for advice."

Gosh, Brad is wise. How often do we let fear keep us from even asking for help? I'm certain that we have all been in those rooms where we feel like we don't belong. We've all had those seemingly crazy ideas that don't see the light of day simply because we are too fearful to raise that flag.

Brad continued, "In the creative field I'm in, I end up having to ask people things like, 'Hey, I have this ice cream truck that we're working on and we're gonna fill it with violinists, and I need help finding them.' All of these weird projects I end up working on that I know I can't do alone.

"I've often felt like, *Oh no, they don't want to hear from me. I don't want to call them. I don't want to interrupt them. I don't want to bother them.* But Madeleine L'Engle had this great phrase she used: *'Do I dare disturb the universe?'* And her answer was 'Yes, disturb the universe, disturb it!'"

Y'all—if someone who has already achieved so much can admit they have fear around calling people up and asking for help, this is good news for the rest of us! We aren't alone, and it's totally normal.

I loved that Brad went on to remind me, "I find that people are so happy to be involved in something where somebody cares. If it's something that you're a little nervous about, but you care about it enough to put in the work, it helps them come alive too. And so I've become more confident disturbing the universe a little bit.

"If I have an idea that scares me and yet it won't go away, that means it's worth pursuing and it's worth inviting people into. They might scratch their heads and be a little confused, but they'll actually be pretty delighted you asked and curious to see it come to life. And maybe it leads somewhere more interesting than you would've been before. But even if it goes sideways, you all end up with a great story and deeper friendships, and that's not too bad."

It seems far too simple to say that the path forward from fear is just to ask for help. And yet I think back to my shark dive. Every person who dove had a guide, a leader who showed us how to breathe, took us through the ropes, and made sure we were safe. Not one of us did it alone.

The key to pushing past fear is to do it scared but, more importantly, not to do it alone.

SELF-ASSESSMENT
• • •

What Do You Need to Unlearn?
- Can you identify places in your work where healthy fear is keeping you from trying something or taking a risk?
- Can you identify something you can do scared?
- When and where should you be bringing in shipmates? When and where should you be asking others for help?

Get Started
How are you approaching healthy fear in your work and leadership? Are you asking for help and making fear your friend? To move forward toward joy and authenticity, you have to start teaching your amygdala who is boss. The next time you feel that prickle of fear creep in, stop and determine what it's trying to keep you from doing. Is it trying to stop you from doing something brave and good or risky and necessary? Your amygdala is going to send the same signals regardless of whether the fear

is healthy or unhealthy. It's up to you to determine whether you choose fight or flight.

CELEBRATE!

Everybody knows something. This is an awesome thing to celebrate! Look at your team structure—chances are that you are surrounded by a wealth of life experience. How can you find ways to share and celebrate that wealth? Are there members of your team who can add insight outside of the roles they are in? Are there shipmates in your organization who can mentor, assist, or make some of those crazy big ideas a reality? Look for the opportunities that already surround you and find ways to celebrate them.

PERFECTION

• • •

Leadership is a practice of imperfect humans leading imperfect humans. That's why it's so hard.
ANNE MORRISS, co-author of *Move Fast and Fix Things*

Y PASSPORT was going to expire. I had been putting off renewing it because every time I remembered, my hair wasn't perfectly done. I'd think, *Oh, I have to get to that. I'll make time at some point and I'll do my hair.* This had been going on for months.

Finally, one morning I got up, printed the form, got in my car, went to the post office, got a photo taken, paid the fee, and mailed in my passport. Done. It took seventeen minutes.

Was my hair perfect? Nope. Did it matter? Nope.

The only people who are going to look at that photo are the people who sit in the airport and look at thousands of photos and will never know me or see me again. So it doesn't matter.

As you move through The Authenticity Map from fear into bravery, the biggest roadblock is often perfection. *But what if it's not ready? What if I'm not good enough? What if I mess it up? What if people see what a mess I really am? What if? What if? What if?*

Perfection is a liar pants. It's a big fat lie that is keeping you from good and great and wonderful and done. The most important part of "do it scared" is not the *scared*. It's the *do it*.

Craig Groeschel, an Oklahoma City pastor and author of *Winning the War in Your Mind*, gave the best advice about overcoming the perfection hang-up. He said that as leaders we typically get stuck in perfectionism because we care deeply about the result of our actions. He added, "But at some point, the return on our efforts or investment will start to diminish—we could do something a little better, but the amount of effort or money it will take isn't worth the increased or improved result." In his team, they use the term "GETMO" to move each other forward. GETMO stands for "good enough to move on."

GETMO has been pretty life-changing for me. My friends and I say it to each other constantly when we see someone getting caught up in perfection paralysis. The saying is true—perfect is the enemy of good. It can also help to adjust our expectations. We can spend all our time worrying and not doing, or we can spend our time doing, learning, and moving forward.

I am a fantastic gift giver. I approach it like an Olympic sport. If you are my friend and you casually mention that you loved this random thing you saw at this random place, I will make it my mission to track that down, wrap it beautifully, and surprise you with it when you least expect it.

But early in my twenties, someone told me, "Val, you have to learn to give the gift without the expectation attached." Once,

I was so excited to give a gift because I just knew the recipient was going to be over the moon. But they weren't. I had put all this time and energy into the searching and buying and wrapping, and their response was lukewarm at best. I was crushed.

I learned that part of the reason I love to give gifts is because of how I feel about the search and wrapping. I needed to not put that same level of expectation on the recipient. When I learned to enjoy the way gifting makes me feel and care less about how it makes the receiver feel, I was free to truly enjoy the giving.

You are going to lead and do and create things—and not everyone is going to feel the same way about them as you do. That doesn't make doing them any less important.

Seth Godin says it best in his blog post "Show Your Work":

> It's tempting to sit in the corner and then, voila, to amaze us all with your perfect answer. But of course, that's not what works. What works is evolving in public, with the team. Showing your work. Thinking out loud. Failing on the way to succeeding, imperfecting on your way to better than good enough.
>
> Ship before you're ready, because you will never be ready. Ready implies you know it's going to work, and you can't know that. You should ship when you're prepared, when it's time to show your work, but not a minute later. The purpose isn't to please the critics. The purpose is to make your work better.

4

BRAVERY
PULL UP
A CHAIR

• • •

*I am a little bit scared. But I am
a lot brave. And the lot brave
part is kicking out the scared part.*

AOIFE DOOLEY, age 4

THE AUTHENTICITY MAP

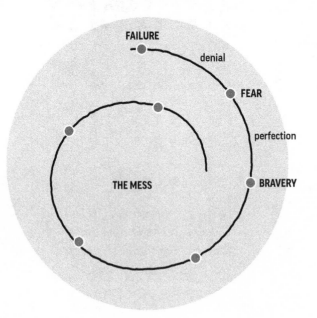

FAILURE

denial

FEAR

perfection

THE MESS

BRAVERY

A FEW YEARS ago, I started taking pottery lessons at a local studio. Throughout my elementary and high school days, art was my happy place. I grew up in a small town with a very small school, but we had a wonderful art department. One day, in grade three, my class visited the high school art room, and we were taught how to make piggy banks in the shape of ducks. I remember the feeling of pinching that clay into a tail and a beak, watching something come to life from a lump of wet earth, and becoming obsessed with the idea of making things.

Over time, my focus turned to drawing and painting, rather than clay. Every free moment I had was spent in the art rooms, and many evenings too, thanks to an art teacher who was super laid-back and let some of us have a key to the back door. (Rumor was he smoked pot in the kiln room, which would probably explain both the reason he was so laid-back and the reason my parents wished I'd spend less time in the art room.)

And then life took over. I left school, and work took up most of my time. I had rent to pay and eventually a mortgage. I got married. I started climbing the corporate ladder. Art became something I never seemed to have time for. My paints dried up. My box of art supplies became a casualty of one of my many moves, and years passed where I never created anything at all. But I never forgot the feeling of pinching that clay into a tail and a beak.

Then the year 2020 happened, and I was a mess. I was grieving and depressed. The world was a dumpster fire. On one fateful day in March, I watched an entire year of speaking engagements collapse like dominoes before my eyes. I had control over nothing.

I spent months that year hiding out. I convinced myself I was staying home because the Centers for Disease Control told us to. But really I was also cowering. I had crawled right back into the failure hole, pitched a tent, forwarded my mail, and gotten super comfy there.

Finally, my therapist told me that I needed to do something, anything, as long as I had to leave the house to do it. So I searched "pottery classes near me" on the internet, and signed up for an eight-week course of evening classes.

We were a motley group. Twelve women and two men. All from different backgrounds and walks of life. Face masks were required, so we smiled nervously with our eyes as we set up our wheel stations that first night. A bucket of water, some basic wooden tools, a sponge, and lumps of medium brown clay.

We worked mostly with reclaim, a clay that is made by mixing all the bits and pieces of many different types of clay. It's similar to the kind of clay you might find straight from the ground—grainy, earthy, with a bit of grit and texture.

After setting up our wheels, we sat in a circle facing the instructor as she patiently explained the basics of wheel throwing. Throwing clay is simply a series of repetitions.

There are a few key steps, and if you get those right, you can create almost anything you can dream up.

First, the clay must be prepped. This is called wedging, and it's similar to kneading dough. The purpose of wedging is to create a smooth egg-shaped ball to begin with and get rid of any air bubbles that might create weaknesses in your finished product.

Then you place the clay on the wheel and begin the process of centering your clay. Your hands apply pressure to the sides of the clay as it spins, creating a cone shape. Next, you apply pressure to the top and sides to compress the clay back into a disc-like shape. This "coning up" and "coning down" process centers the clay on the wheel. If you cannot master this step, it's nearly impossible to proceed any further.

Once your clay is centered, you can open it up. Your thumbs create a dip or hole in the middle and ultimately form the base of whatever you are making.

Finally, the clay needs to be moved up the sides of the piece to make the walls or sides of whatever you are making. The process of moving the clay upwards is called "pulling the walls."

If you can master wedging, centering, opening, and pulling, you can create anything—bowls, cups, vases, etc. The movements are the same; the only differences are how much clay you use and the shapes you manipulate the clay into.

Up. Down. Out. Up.

That is all there is to wheel throwing. It sounds so simple. The instructor made it look so simple. And I was terrible at it.

I spent the next eight weeks simply trying to get the hang of centering. While my classmates moved on to more complex techniques, I spent class after class doing the same repetitive movements, trying to form a consistent cone that I could open and pull. Even when I did create something that looked halfway decent, when I got to the trimming stage—cleaning and smoothing the piece after it was dried and before it went to the kiln—I would find that it was still not centered and therefore would trim unevenly. In short, everything I made was wonky.

I left class each week frustrated and a little embarrassed about my stubby bowls that resembled ashtrays made by a child. Week after week, I would toss my efforts in the bucket of failed attempts, to be turned back into reclaim for future weeks.

But when the eight-week class ended, I signed up for another one. And then another. Even though I didn't feel like I was progressing. While others moved on to advanced classes, I stayed in the beginner class, joined by a brand-new group of people every two months, going through the most basic instructions again and again.

Until one day, the instructor assigned me a speed drill. Five-minute sprints in which to throw a cylinder or bowl. My task was to do four in a row without a pause. Four pieces in twenty minutes.

"Speed drills? How is that going to help me?" I asked.

She smiled and replied, "Because it will force you to get out of your head and stop overthinking. When you don't take extra time to stress or worry, you will simply do the motions that you've been taught. You'll do what you know works."

It was a lightbulb moment.

That day, I learned that it was easier when I was brave enough to speed up. When I hesitated, I made more mistakes. I was trying to make it look good, rather than doing the repetitions that I'd been taught. In pottery, it's actually easier if you keep moving and better if you pick up the pace.

All those months, I thought the lesson was "be brave enough to suck at something new." But the lesson really was much more straightforward. When you don't know what to do—do what you know.

Bravery, I think, is where authenticity truly begins and where joy truly becomes possible. We may start in failure and have to navigate fear, but bravery is where we get to the good stuff. But, just like in pottery class, it's also where we often get stuck trying to make things look good and forgetting to do what we know.

• • •

A SEAT AT THE TABLE

The first time I got a seat at the table, I was just twenty-four years old. I had been hired as an administrator for the volunteer services department of the American Red Cross, based in Western New York. It was just a year after 9/11, and the country was still feeling the patriotic aftermath.

I interviewed with a rather stern woman who scared me a bit. And on the morning of my first day, I learned that she had resigned the week before. The details of what followed are a bit fuzzy, but instead of becoming her administrative assistant, I found myself replacing her as director of the entire department. It was the first time I had a private office with an actual door.

I had five years of experience in administration. I had managed people, projects, and tasks. I was organized, determined, and creative. But I was woefully unprepared for the job in which I found myself.

• • •

When you don't know
what to do—do what you know.

• • •

As director, I was responsible for recruiting and organizing hundreds of volunteers for dozens of events each month. We needed people to staff fundraisers, coordinate blood drives, set up and take down event equipment, answer phones, provide disaster services, teach first aid, participate in any number of administrative tasks, and train other volunteers. Not one of those people was paid or compensated in any way. My role was basically to beg people to work for free.

As with any nonprofit or charitable organization, oversight was provided by a board of directors and trustees. There was a committee for everything, and everything had to go through a committee to move forward. But I was young, impatient, and terribly green—and the pace of decisions frustrated me. I wasn't diplomatic. I didn't have the negotiation skills to ask for what I needed. I wanted desperately to look good and be important. And in my first meeting with the executive director of the chapter, in a moment of sheer exasperation, I shouted at her. It would be the last time I had a seat at that table, and I would spend the rest of my time in that role working on menial tasks until I finally resigned.

As leaders, we spend a lot of time, consciously or unconsciously, arranging tables and chairs.

The goal always seems to be a seat at the table. The table is where decisions are made. Careers are made (or unmade). Voices are heard (or dismissed). But it all starts and ends at the table.

Getting to "the table" has been a topic of conversation for generations. It has even deeper meaning for people of color, who literally fought (and continue to fight) for a seat at the table, as referenced in Langston Hughes's iconic poem "I, Too." As the poem goes,

> Tomorrow,
> I'll be at the table
> When company comes.
> Nobody'll dare
> Say to me,
> "Eat in the kitchen,"
> Then.

And for women, getting a seat at the table has long meant breaking the glass ceiling and breaking past the "boys club" barriers that have long existed in our workplaces. For many of us, it's a struggle to just get to the table.

I was chatting with my friend Valerie Alexander, a gifted writer, speaker, and CEO of Speak Happiness, and I asked her what is keeping so many of us from a seat at that proverbial table. Her response caught me off guard. "I think what keeps us from asking for a place at the table is not even knowing that there is a table," she said.

She went on to say, "I've been a CEO, a filmmaker, an author, a lawyer, an investment banker, and a keynote speaker. But when I graduated from college, of all those jobs, I'd only ever heard of lawyer and author. And I didn't think I could make money as an author, so I became a lawyer. But after I became a lawyer, I was a venture capital consultant. I never heard of venture capital and didn't even know consulting was a profession. Before I was an investment banker, I had no idea what investment bankers did. I'd never heard of that either. Later I became a screenwriter. I guess I knew people wrote movies and I assumed got paid for them, but it didn't occur to me that that was somebody's job."

Valerie told me about a time when she was working as a lawyer on a deal with some investment bankers from Montgomery Securities, and one of them said to her, "God, Valerie, with the way your mind works, you should really be an analyst."

She explained that in investment banking, there are two kinds of analysts. The most junior, internship-level people are called analysts. She had been seeing them proofreading and getting coffee. So when her boss, the partner at the law firm, made a face and said, "You don't want to be an analyst," Valerie was looking at these junior interns thinking, *Yeah, I don't want that.*

But what she didn't know is that in investment banking, there's a different role with the title of analyst. That person researches everything about an industry and its space, gets to know all the companies, has conversations with the

CEOs, flies all over the world, and is not only one of the most important but one of the most highly paid members of the firm.

Valerie continued, "At the time in the internet space, the analyst at Montgomery Securities was an extremely powerful and well-respected woman, and if I had even twice considered what they were saying and said, 'Really? What do you mean?' I might have had a meeting with her. Three years later, when I became an investment banker, the investment bank I joined didn't have an internet analyst and we hired a guy who didn't have anywhere near the financial analysis skills I did. But it turns out he had been the guy who went to work for her, and that's why he got that job and, get this, a million-dollar signing bonus. And that's a career trajectory I might have had."

It's sobering to think that such a small thing is often standing between us and the opportunities that we want most.

"So you need the bravery and the willingness to ask the questions," Valerie told me. "You don't have to throw yourself under the bus to do it. You don't have to say, 'Oh, I'm so stupid. I don't know what that means.' But I would've had a much different career and a much bigger place at the table if I had known what the chairs at the table were even for."

. . .

GETTING TO THE TABLE

After my experience with the Red Cross, it took me years to find my way. I knew that I wanted to grow in my role as a leader and have bigger opportunities to impact change, but getting to the table was a challenge for me. Every time I saw an opportunity to advance, the bravery required to ask the right questions held me back. Often, I didn't even realize that was the problem.

I was raised to work hard. "If you see something that needs to be done, don't wait for someone else to do it" was frequently repeated when I was growing up. As an employee, I applied the same thought process. If I just worked hard enough, did enough, and took on enough, I assumed I would eventually be given the opportunities I wanted. But the only thing that seemed to get me was a plate overflowing with tasks no one else wanted and a growing frustration with my work. I was leading others, but I wasn't using my skills or talents, and I was growing increasingly resentful.

"Ask for what you want" always felt like an ick for me. It didn't come naturally, and I wasn't good at it. So I watched as time and time again, someone equally or less qualified than I was would be given a raise, an opportunity, or a role that I would have wanted.

I remember a day after a particularly frustrating employee review where I was again passed over for something that excited me. I vented for a good solid hour to my friend before she looked at me and said, "Well, did you ask for that opportunity?"

I recall sputtering with frustration. They should have known! Look at all the work I was doing! Look at all the hours I was putting in! Clearly, I was ready for these bigger roles!

My friend just blinked at me and laughed. "But how will they know what you want if you never ask for it?" It was the

BRAVERY: PULL UP A CHAIR   **87**

most obvious answer, and it had never occurred to me to do it. The very next day I walked into the office and asked for the opportunity I wanted. My boss responded with surprise, telling me they had no idea that's what I wanted because I seemed so busy and happy in my current role.

Over the next decade, I learned three critical steps about asking.

First, don't assume people can read your mind. (This one has been a general life lesson that can apply to almost every circumstance in my life, and it's likely the one thing that keeps my therapist in business. Sigh.) It's true. People are not mind readers. They aren't going to magically know what you want unless you say it.

Second, be brave enough to go big. In most cases, you won't get more than what you're willing to ask for, so don't water down your ask for fear of getting a no. Think about your ideal outcome and then courageously ask for it. Show that you understand your own value. While you may not always get exactly what you want, you'll almost always end up with more than if you hadn't been bold in your request.

Third, be specific. I went from hoping for a seat at a table to asking for a specific seat at a specific table with specific responsibilities. As Tim Ferriss says, "Life punishes the vague wish and rewards the specific ask." The clearer I became about what I wanted and what I could accomplish, the more specific my requests became.

Getting to the table is one thing. Getting what you want once you are there is entirely another. Once I had a seat at the table, I had to unlearn some big lies I'd been telling myself about negotiation.

In their book, *Women Don't Ask,* Linda Babcock and Lara Laschever explore the barriers holding women back when negotiating. Their research highlights the continued gender divide when it comes to asking.

Men initiate negotiations about four times as often as women.

Women are more pessimistic about how much is available when they do negotiate and so they typically ask for and get less when they do negotiate—on average, 30 percent less than men.

Twenty percent of adult women say they never negotiate at all, even though they often recognize negotiation as appropriate and even necessary.

The Institute for Women's Policy Research found that women in the United States earned only about 83 percent of men's median annual earnings in 2021. Also, "Compared to the median weekly earnings of White men working full-time, Hispanic women's full-time earnings were just 58.4 percent, Black women's 63.1 percent, and White women's 79.6 percent."

At the core of this are some deeply ingrained societal gender roles. Girls are encouraged and expected from an early age to be accommodating and care about others more than themselves. Whereas boys are taught to be assertive, competitive, and profit-oriented. This leads to it being more acceptable for men to negotiate hard for themselves, while women are more likely to be seen as troublesome and pushy.

In the workplace, female negotiators often get penalized for negotiating more assertively because they are deviating from gender stereotypes, regularly getting worse outcomes rather than better ones. Simply teaching women to negotiate better won't fix the problem. Instead, we all have to become more aware of our biases and stop perpetrating them.

. . .

Getting to the table is one thing.

Getting what you want once

you are there is entirely another.

. . .

I asked Valerie Alexander about this. Her work on unconscious bias was the subject of her book *How Women Can Succeed in the Workplace (Despite Having "Female Brains")*. "We tell people, particularly women, to just negotiate better," she said. "But you're not negotiating in a void. You are negotiating with a person who has a certain set of beliefs and expectations and parameters and only so much of their own political capital to go fight for you to get more.

"One of the things I share with women is you have to have the pre-negotiation conversation. Say, 'Hey, I am very excited about this opportunity'—because God forbid a woman not present herself as excited. You know, we never expect men to be excited about jobs. We never expect men to be grateful for the opportunity, but somehow women are supposed to be those two things. So, fine. Get out in front of it. Say, 'I'm really excited about this opportunity. One thing I'm most excited about is that I know this company won't hold it against me when I negotiate for more money, which happens to many women.' This allows you to disempower their bias by acknowledging it."

Once we address the bias, Valerie says, we also have to unlearn the way we pre-negotiate with ourselves. And this was the big one for me. This was the hurdle that held me back for years.

"First off, don't ever negotiate against yourself. So don't start by thinking, *I really should get two hundred thousand dollars for this, but they're never going to give me that. You know what, I'll start by asking for a hundred and fifty thousand.* Do not negotiate against yourself upfront. Do your research and know the market value of what you're doing. Do the research and know your worth."

I didn't just have to unlearn the unwritten rules of negotiation; I had to unlearn the lie that I'd told myself for years—that I wasn't allowed to have more. That I should be grateful for what I had and to want more was greedy and selfish.

It was the author of *A Return to Love*, Marianne Williamson, who changed this for me, when she wrote, "Your playing small does not serve the world." I realized I didn't just want bigger roles or responsibilities. I wanted to impact more people. Create more change. Help more humans. It wasn't about me; it was about what those roles allowed me to do for others.

This was perhaps the biggest turning point for me on my way from failure and fear into authenticity and joy. I was allowed to ask for more. I was allowed to ask for what I wanted. And I was allowed to do it bravely and purposefully. I had to write myself that permission slip, and I truly believe that learning this lesson is what ultimately turned me into a leader.

. . .

PULL UP CHAIRS

The trailblazing New York congresswoman Shirley Chisholm told us back in the 1970s, "If they don't give you a seat at the table, bring a folding chair."

I have always loved that battle cry, but as Valerie Alexander reminded me "The person sitting in the folding chair does not always have a voice at the table."

The real role of a leader isn't to simply be at the table; it's to pull up chairs for others and make sure their voices are heard. For me, this is where bravery continues to play the biggest role. It's about getting people to the table who don't look, think, or sound like the voices that are already there. It's about challenging the "this is how we've always done things" people with an earnest and sincere "But why?"

This hasn't always made me the most popular person in the room. As a speaker, I have turned down opportunities to speak because event organizers have stacked the agenda with those who all look and believe the same way. I have left organizations and opportunities for the same reason. I have spoken out when there are no women or people of color on stage or represented at the tables where decisions are made.

Brave leadership is about getting others to the table, pulling up chairs, and saying, "Can y'all scooch over just a bit?" And when all else fails, it's about building your own table.

The hardest lesson of all is learning that sometimes you must leave the table you desperately wanted to sit at to find a table where you can make the most difference.

This is a significant enough truth, especially for women of color, that it makes headlines when the only Black female CEO to run an S&P 500 company resigns. (For example, when Rosalind Brewer, former CEO of Walgreens, resigned in September 2023.) Getting to the table is tough, and once you get there, it can be lonely. Especially when you are the only one who looks or believes as you do.

Authentic, brave leadership is doing what you know. It's knowing when to ask the questions and learning how to ask for what you want. It's knowing when to leave the table or build your own. But most importantly, it's about adding chairs for others.

Some of the messiest moments at work happen around the table. But you are never going to be at the right table at the right time until you give yourself permission to be there, to be yourself, and to do what you know.

SELF-ASSESSMENT
• • •

What Do You Need to Unlearn?

- What are the basic steps you should be returning to when you don't know what to do?
- How are you diminishing your ask before you even make it?
- Where do you get stuck trying to make things look good, instead of doing what you know?
- If you are already at the table, how can you pull up chairs for others?

Get Started

In pottery, the way I know if I'm improving is by making something and then ripping it apart.

The outside of the piece might look perfect, but the inside tells the real story. It tells me if I got out the air bubbles or made the walls an even thickness—things that could ruin a pot once it's exposed to extreme heat in the kiln. Every time I'm tempted to sit back and feel like I've made it, I am reminded that until I'm willing to dismantle a process, rip open my habits, and take a close look at my assumptions, I might just be looking at a super shiny facade that isn't going to survive the fire.

It sucks to throw a bunch of nice-looking bowls and then cut them in half. But I've learned so much by being brave enough to do it. And over time, I (hopefully) will stop making the same mistakes. What are some of the assumptions you may need to rip open in order to become a more courageous leader?

CELEBRATE!

If pottery taught me anything, it's that the process is often more important than the result. Look for ways to celebrate the process with your team or in your work. The process is where we work those consistency muscles, take risks, and show up at the table. It's also where we are going to learn more about what each of the chairs at that table is for. It's not always about making the finished product look good. Celebrate the steps you took to get there.

SHAME

• • •

The willingness to show up changes us.
It makes us a little braver each time.

BRENÉ BROWN, *Daring Greatly*

A s WE start showing up, speaking up, and leading bravely, it's almost a guarantee that we'll encounter the ugliest roadblock of them all.

Shame is one of the driving forces of how we show up in this world. It's a key emotion in the human experience. While guilt is often about specific behaviors, shame is about identity. It tells us that what we have done *defines us* and becomes us.

What will people think? What will they say? Have I tried too hard? Am I too much? Am I enough?

This roadblock can send us right back to failure and defeat and *I suck, everything sucks, it will always suck*—but only if we let it.

In her TED Talk, Brené Brown says, "If you put shame in a petri dish, it needs three ingredients to grow exponentially: secrecy, silence, and judgment. If you put the same amount of shame in the petri dish and douse it with empathy, it can't survive."

When we start to feel the shame spiral circling, we must find ways to remove the secrecy, silence, and judgment.

First, recognize it. Call it what it is. Instead of saying, "I suck. I screwed up. I am such a failure," recognize that the shame you are feeling doesn't define you. Just as fear is a distress response from your amygdala, shame is also a result of chemicals swirling through your brain. It doesn't need to define you, and you don't have to wear it around as your identity.

Second, reach out and talk about it. Vulnerability is hard. I get it. But the more you are willing to show your mess, the more others will gather around and support you. Shame was the reason I found myself sobbing in that utility closet. I was afraid to show my mess. I was terrified that others would judge me or write me off. But the moment that I started to lay my mess on the table and gather people around me, the shame started to dissipate. As Brené Brown says, "If we can share our story with someone who responds with empathy and understanding, shame can't survive."

B.T. Harman, a creator, consultant, and author of *Blue Babies Pink*, once said, "The people with the best stories are not the ones who sit around talking about how awesome their lives are. They are the ones who are open about their screwups, their embarrassing moments, their idiosyncrasies, and their hidden secrets that cause us to say, 'OMG, ME TOO.' People would rather see our sincere struggle than our polished perfection. As it turns out, there is a reward for vulnerability. For inviting people in to see the parts of our story that we fear are unlovely, injured, or in process. That reward is trust."

5

CURIOSITY
SAYING
HARD THINGS

• • •

To live a creative life, we must
lose our fear of being wrong.

JOSEPHINE BAKER, American-born French dancer,
singer, and actress

THE AUTHENTICITY MAP

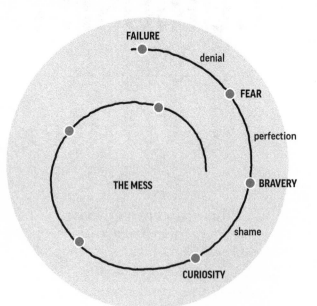

FAILURE

denial

FEAR

perfection

THE MESS

BRAVERY

shame

CURIOSITY

WITH CURIOSITY, we come to my favorite part of The Authenticity Map. We've moved out of failure and fear, past denial and shame, and we've started embracing bravery. This is where it starts getting good! We are moving into the happier-sounding emotions. Curiosity, hooray!

I loved the Curious George books when I was a kid. How could you not love stories about a cheeky monkey who was always getting in hot water because of his sense of curiosity? My favorite was one of the original stories, *Curious George Rides a Bike*. In the story, the Man in the Yellow Hat gives George a blue bicycle, which George uses to help the local paperboy deliver his papers. In true Curious George fashion, chaos ensues as his curiosity leads him from one mishap to another. In the end, the Man in the Yellow Hat shows up, all the mix-ups are resolved, and everyone lives happily ever after. (At least until the next book.)

As children, curiosity is a critical part of learning about the world around us. We are encouraged to ask questions about everything, so we ask why the sky is blue, why our hands have fingers but our feet have toes, and where pets go when they die. It's seen as adorable and endearing.

As we grow older, we are told to ask questions when we don't know something. Hiring managers drill this into us as a desirable skill. The ability to ask questions is seen as a positive attribute in a new employee, proving that you are coachable and attentive.

But at some point, this attitude toward curiosity seems to change. We are supposed to know. To be sure. To have the answers. As we move into more senior positions of leadership, we tend to replace our curiosity with certainty. We want to look like we know what we are doing. We need people to trust us. And somewhere along the way, curiosity goes from being something adorable and endearing to being seen as annoying and a waste of time.

Einstein is arguably one of the greatest minds of all time. He developed the theory of relativity and is maybe best known for his discovery of the mass-energy equivalence formula (we know it as $E = mc^2$). But he's also the man who said, "I've no special talents. I am only passionately curious." He attributed all of his work—accomplishments that are almost too great to name—to his curiosity.

In 2018, Francesca Gino conducted a study for *Harvard Business Review* on curiosity in the workplace. Gino found that curiosity is vital to an organization's performance. It improves engagement and collaboration and helps people make better choices. Workplaces that encouraged curiosity also had fewer errors, more innovation in both creative and noncreative jobs, reduced group conflict, more open communication, and better team performance. However, Gino surveyed more than three thousand employees from a wide range of firms and industries and found that only about 24 percent reported feeling curious in their jobs on a regular basis.

She also found that while leaders might say they value creative thinkers and question-askers, in reality, most leaders stifle curiosity for fear that it will increase risk and lead to inefficiency.

In other words, we don't *really* want to embrace curiosity. We don't *really* want our team members to go down rabbit holes or start chasing squirrels. We want positive predictions, clear numbers, goals that can be met, and measurable growth. We want certainty.

And yet, if we want to be joyful leaders, we must be brave enough to step out of fear and embrace uncertainty. We have to foster an environment that allows for and encourages curiosity. And just like in the Curious George books, we have to allow for the chaos that may follow.

. . .

UNLEARNING CERTAINTY

I used to hate meetings. Like, I really, really hated them. I would sit in meetings and grit my teeth, willing them to be over. I preferred going to the dentist over sitting in meetings.

I was working in senior leadership at RE/MAX, LLC at this point, and one of the perks of the job was access to Dan Coughlin, a leadership coach. I told Dan about my hatred of meetings, and he laughed. Then he realized I was serious. I could understand his disbelief. We spend most of our early careers trying to get seats at the table for important meetings... and then we spend the rest of our careers trying to get out of them. Hashtag ironic.

I told him that I spent most meetings sitting there listening to the ideas being shared and all I could think about were the ways each idea would fail.

"Hang on," he said. "You sit in meetings day after day and all you think about is how ideas will *fail*?"

It was true. I hadn't even realized I was doing it until I said it out loud. I thought I was doing the right thing. I was looking for the single best solution, but in the process, I was shutting off the faucet of ideas that might lead to an even better one. That day, Dan gave me some homework that would change my life. He told me to sit in my meetings over the next several weeks and for every idea that was shared, he wanted me to think of one way it *could* work.

I am not going to lie—this took practice. The search for certainty over curiosity was so ingrained in me that I had to fight it every step of the way. My first instinct when someone would suggest a solution was to immediately shut it down. Retraining my brain to replace "but" with "what if" took time and effort.

In her research on curiosity, Francesca Gino found that the best way to foster a more curious environment at work was to ask questions like, "Why?" "What if...?" and "How might we...?"

My friend Brad Montague, who often speaks to children, tells a story of how he conducts this exercise in his work at elementary schools. He seats the students in a circle and asks them a series of three questions.

First, he asks, "*I wonder who we could help?*" In childlike fashion, they brainstorm all kinds of options. The janitor! The librarian! Jimmy from the class next door! Then Brad asks them, "*I wonder what's the most amazing thing we could do for them*?" Cue more outrageous brainstorming. Balloons! Elephants! A song! And finally, Brad asks, "*I wonder who could help us*?" This is where they get to the good stuff. Perhaps a teacher or an adult could help them make these amazing things a reality.

Children are born with curiosity. But as an adult, I had to unlearn certainty in order to find curiosity in my work. And once I did, I became a far more authentic leader. Instead of sitting in meetings grinding my teeth, I started to find the joy in *not knowing*. I began to ask myself:

> What if that idea did work?
> What if we added on to that and we did this thing too?
> And what if that led to us doing this and this and this?

Did things get messy? Yes. My team took more risks. I remember hearing my manager describe one particular risk as "a failure before it even began," when he thought I was out of earshot. His comment lit a fire under me that would lead to career opportunities I could have never imagined.

. . .

Children are born with curiosity.

But as an adult, I had to unlearn certainty

in order to find curiosity in my work.

. . .

But, most importantly, curiosity became a habit. When failure did happen, I spent less time in shame and fear and got to bravery and curiosity (and ultimately joy) faster, because I didn't need to know exactly what would happen next. I spent less time planning for certainty and more time doing, risking, and learning.

● ● ●

PLAN LESS, DO MORE

I have always been a huge fan of the organization World Central Kitchen. In 2010, chef José Andrés traveled to Haiti following a devastating earthquake. He set up temporary kitchens to cook alongside displaced families and was guided on the proper way to cook black beans the way Haitians like to eat them. For José, it wasn't just about feeding people in need—it was about listening, learning, and cooking side by side with the people impacted. This meaning of comfort food is the core value that José, along with his wife, Patricia, placed at the center of World Central Kitchen's mission.

For several years, the organization focused on longer-term solutions around food in the Caribbean and Central America. But José never forgot about those early days cooking in the camp in Haiti. In 2017, Hurricane Harvey hit Houston, and José, with several chefs from his team, decided it was time to act. They landed in Houston and began helping to prepare meals. José immediately saw gaps and ways that food handling during a crisis could be improved. Just a month later, Hurricane Maria hit Puerto Rico, bringing catastrophic devastation, and millions of Americans were in immediate need. Boarding the first commercial flight to San Juan, José started with one kitchen, at a friend's restaurant. Building fast, chefs, food trucks, and volunteers joined the team. WCK would go on to serve nearly four million fresh meals in the aftermath of Maria.

Driven by their belief that food is a universal human right, WCK teams have served meals to people recovering from crises every single day since. The way José Andrés and his team show up anywhere and everywhere to feed people after natural disasters is both inspiring and mind-blowing.

Partnering with local restaurants and cooks, they prepare meals with whatever ingredients are available, learning to make food the way the locals like to eat it. In the WCK cookbook, they talk about how one of the core tenets (and running jokes) at WCK is that they don't have meetings and they don't plan. They just start cooking. José Andrés is known for saying, "You can't tell a hurricane which way to turn; all you can do is *react* to that turn."

Planning isn't a bad thing, exactly. Most organizations spend thousands of hours each year in meetings trying to plan for every possible outcome. However, always planning and never doing is a recipe for a weak business that is unable to change course when the hurricane does come. We learn best by doing, not by planning. Plans can help us stay focused and on budget, but doing is where we learn the most valuable lessons about what works and what doesn't.

At some point, you simply have to start cooking. And you may have to do that before you have all the ingredients, or before you even know where they will come from. There is a certain magic that comes from being willing to take action in uncertainty.

. . .

FEED ME TACOS AND TELL ME I'M PRETTY

I didn't just have to learn to apply curiosity in meetings. I had to learn to apply it to myself.

Once we start showing up bravely at work, inevitably, we receive feedback and criticism. We receive questions and pushback. We say the things and people respond. This is another area where I had to unlearn certainty.

I don't recall my first employee review. But I remember my last one like it was yesterday: "Needs to work on taking negative feedback less personally."

Of about seven pages of positive comments, that one point stood out like a flashing neon sign. It wasn't wrong. This was an area where I applied certainty liberally, like guac on tacos. I could ignore the positive, constructive stuff like a boss and focus entirely on the one or two negative comments. I'd roll them around in my head, hold them close, and snuggle up to them at night—sure that they were true and that I was a total failure.

And then one day, on a live Facebook video, I heard author Glennon Doyle talk about feedback in a way I'd never heard before. She described the act of putting your voice and your work into the world as if you were putting a letter into a mailbox. For every letter you mail, you'll get a hundred letters in response. Those letters represent feedback.

Glennon said that when a man puts his work into the world, the question he usually faces is "Is his work worthy?" But when a woman puts her work into the world, the question is most often "Is she worthy of putting out work?" Most of the criticism we receive will be about us, and not about our work. This is why it will feel personal. "If you put your work into the world," she said, "you have to learn to sort your mail."

Of those one hundred letters of feedback, the first forty letters you receive will be about your appearance. What you look like. If you are too thin or too fat or too tall or too short, or they don't like your hair, etc. "Does your appearance have anything to do with your work?" Glennon asks. If not, *junk mail.*

The next thirty will be about your relationships, basing your worthiness on your roles, your standing with other people, your position as spouses, siblings, parents, bosses, etc. Don't ask, "Is this true?" Instead, ask, "Am I am in relationships with these people?" If not, *junk mail.*

The next twenty will be about your personality. You are too dramatic, anxious, depressed, happy, preachy, clueless, loud, etc. Ask yourself, "Is my personality up for feedback?" If not, *junk mail.*

The next ten pieces of mail will actually be about your work. Look through them. Six will be nasty, personal, and mean. "But," Glennon says, "we don't take criticism from people who don't know how to communicate." So, *junk mail.*

That leaves four letters. Four pieces of feedback out of one hundred. These letters are about the real work. They are thoughtful. They may offer a new perspective. They might be critical. And they may hurt because they are real. Glennon says, "These letters I bring inside. I read them over and over. I let them hurt. And I let them change me. Teach me. Help me know better so I can do better. That's the good stuff."

Sort your mail. This single reminder changed the way I handled feedback. I learned to be curious instead of certain.

Instead of holding the negative feedback close and being certain it was true, I learned to sit with it and ask questions. As Glennon advised, I started with these questions:

Is this about my appearance?
Is this about my personality?
Am I in a relationship with this person?
Is this someone I would take advice from?
Does this sting because it is true and important and real?

Being curious about feedback is one of the most important parts of communication. It can also be the toughest. Maya Angelou said, "The real difficulty is to overcome how you think about yourself."

As a speaker, I have gotten more than my fair share of feedback. I stand on stage and talk for a living. My words are never going to resonate with everyone. I have gotten emails telling me I changed their lives. I have also gotten messages saying that I was terribly unimpressive. I've often thought, *How can both of those things be true?* But they are.

• • •

GETTING FEEDBACK

Jon Acuff, the author of *Soundtracks: The Surprising Solution to Overthinking* and *All It Takes Is a Goal,* once told a story on stage about a time he asked his wife, Jenny, about something he had written. Jenny responded, "Do you want compliments or feedback?" (A wise woman, that Jenny.)

As leaders, we are going to get comments, feedback, and criticism—whether we like it or not. So, why not ask for it? The key is to ask for what we need and learn to ask for it in a way that will be helpful.

I once worked with a creative director who told clients, "We don't want your feedback—we want your direction." At first that sounded rather harsh, but it was hella effective. Instead of hearing "Well, I don't like that shade of blue," we received specific direction such as "Make it darker."

As a young employee, I craved constructive feedback. I wanted to know how I could improve and what I could do better. I wasn't alone. In a recent study, 72 percent of employees rated "managers providing critical feedback" as important for them in career development, but only 5 percent believed their managers provided such feedback. There is a whole host of reasons why we may not get the feedback we need—but the quickest remedy is to ask for it.

This is one area where I had to learn to implement strategic curiosity. Rather than asking, "Do you have any feedback on that work?" I learned to ask more specific and open-ended questions. For example, "What would you like to see more of?" or "What specific changes would you make?"

As a speaker, if someone stops me after a talk to say, "Great job," I try to ask, "What resonated with you?" or "What is the one thing that stood out most for you?" Compliments are nice, and we all love to receive them, but they aren't going to help us improve.

It's also important that we give people the words we want them to use. I have a speaker friend who was lamenting how her clients always call her a "facilitator" instead of a "speaker." So I asked her, "Have you given them those words about you? Have you introduced yourself as a speaker when you are working with them?"

The thing is... we usually only ever get what we ask for. As Brené Brown says, "Clear is kind." You'll get the best feedback when you are the most specific and clear about what kind of feedback you want, why you want it, and how you will use it.

• • •

GIVING FEEDFORWARD

I once had a boss who constantly said that dreaded line, "Don't come to me with problems, come to me with solutions." While he intended to encourage his team to think about how we might solve the challenges we faced, it made him unapproachable in the times we needed him most. The one lesson I took from that was to never be afraid to have my team come to me for what they needed.

While I love to ask for feedback, when I am giving it, I like to think of it as feedforward. I love this term because it feels like we're moving the project forward, passing the ball, or making progress. It also makes the recipient feel less defensive. Feedforward is most effective when it's not a download of my feelings but is actionable and constructive.

In his book, *Rhythm: How to Achieve Breakthrough Execution and Accelerate Growth*, author Patrick Thean writes, "The first piece of advice I like to give to new leaders is: Feedback is love. Feedback isn't some scary monster out to destroy the self-esteem of your team and make them hate you. Instead, I like to think of giving and receiving useful feedback as a bond-builder that creates relationships able to weather the storms."

I asked my friend Jessica Swesey for her thoughts on feedback and feedforward. A gifted writer, editor, and partner at the branding firm 1000watt, Jessica might be one of the best I know at this. I have watched her mull something over and then speak clearly, succinctly, and kindly—giving direction that both empowers the listener and addresses the problem. It's like watching a choreographed dance.

She said, "Before I give feedback, I put myself in their shoes. If I was doing something that could be better, wouldn't I want to know? When it's feedback about a piece of writing, for example, you just have to remember that there's me, there's you, and then there's the piece of writing, and it's separate. So let's try to create some neutrality around it. I think it's always helpful to be specific without being too prescriptive because then you're not giving the person the ability to solve the problem on their own."

Great salespeople know that one of the most valuable parts of the sales transaction is the client testimonial. The problem is that too many salespeople wait until the transaction is over to ask for it. The best and most constructive testimonials come when you ask midstream. In the middle of a stressful negotiation or when emotions are involved. This is when you get the most honest and real responses— responses that will help you to learn and grow, as well as showcase what you are capable of.

As leaders, we should never be saving up our feedback or feedforward for an annual review. At that point, it's almost too late. The emotions have gone or have simmered into resentment or, worse, indifference. If you get to annual reviews and your team members are surprised by something that comes up, you have let them down.

The greatest gifts a leader can give are recognition and feedforward. These both show that you are paying attention and want them to succeed. Learning to let go of my certainty in this area (*I know what the problem is, or why they are behaving this way*) and starting with curiosity (*I wonder what they are struggling with or how I can help?*) was the key to approaching feedforward with an open mind.

In terms of accepting or taking on the feedback, criticism, and opinions of others, this is yet another area to surrender the certainty. Just because someone says it doesn't make it true. Even if that someone is a person you respect.

You get to decide who you travel with. We get to decide who we give our headspace to. We all get to decide which pieces of advice and feedback we put into our backpacks and carry with us throughout our lives and careers. Pack your bags wisely, friends. The wrong choices can unnecessarily weigh you down for years.

As Jessica reminded me, "You don't have to take all feedback. Generally, I like to be open to it, but sometimes it's fine to just reject it. Others don't always know better than you. I've had to remember that it's okay to disagree."

Junk mail: We don't have to take on all the feedback we are given. And we don't have to respond to it all either.

• • •

EVEN WHEN YOUR VOICE SHAKES

I have never been one to hold back on sharing my opinions. (I come by it honestly. My Grams is nearly a hundred, and *she's* never held back a day in her life.) But over time, I have learned to temper my certainty. I am not always right, nor am I always the one who must save the world.

I do believe, however, that authentic leaders are not silent in tough times. Just as it's our role to sometimes give constructive feedback, it's also our responsibility to speak up and say the hard things.

A few years ago, I was contracted to speak at an event. Over three days, this conference would strive to help a large audience of leaders find solutions to their most pressing recruiting and retention challenges. Weeks after I signed the contract, the full event agenda was published. On the speaker list, there were seventeen men (all over the age of fifty), two women, and zero persons of color.

This speaker list did not reflect the audience. The attendees were people of all ages, genders, races, and backgrounds. They led teams that were even more diverse. And yet the people taking the stage were primarily from a single demographic. I wondered how the event would be able to successfully speak to the various nuances and challenges this audience faced, and I voiced this concern to the event organizers. The pushback was swift and defensive. I was uninvited to speak and my contract was canceled.

Being a lone voice of dissent or a single voice raising uncomfortable questions is never fun. But this is one area where curiosity and bravery go hand in hand. And this is a critical part of becoming an authentic leader.

Authenticity often means saying the hard things. The things that perhaps no one else will say. Coming at them from a place of curiosity instead of certainty can offer a safe space for others to come alongside you. As Francesca Gino suggested in her *Harvard Business Review* study, using questions like "Why?" "What if…?" and "How might we…?" allows others to broach touchy subjects with bravery. If you approach having tough conversations with curiosity, you may find new ways to connect and move forward together.

• • •

We all get to decide which pieces of advice
and feedback we put into our backpacks and carry
with us throughout our lives and careers.

• • •

In their book, *Speak Up*, Megan Reitz and John Higgins write, "There are no top five lists to speaking truth to power. There is no prescription, instead each of us has to find our own way of making this possible in the unique contexts that we find ourselves, dealing with the individual and collective histories that are alive in the world. As soon as we reach for the boiled down checklist, we will inevitably strip away the liveliness that makes it possible for the relationships, within which we all know and find our identity, to be worked with to shift their established patterns."

I think that is a fancy way of saying there is no easy button for these situations. And he's right. His quote, "Walking toward the sound of disagreement is what gives an organization vitality," is such a profound way to remind us that an organization is stronger and more joyful when we can have hard conversations.

One of the reasons we get into hot water at work when we speak truth to power is not because of what we say, but how we say it. When we come in with brimstone and judgment, instead of empathy and curiosity, we are less likely to get our desired result. We have to take the time to build relationships based on our desire not to simply fix the problem but to also see others succeed.

I think back to the event where I was supposed to speak. It wasn't the last time I've been added to a similar speaker lineup. But these days, I respond differently. Instead of asking the event organizer how they intend to meet the diverse needs of their audience, I help them do it. I suggest other speakers. Make introductions. Bring others into the conversation. I approach it with curiosity instead of certainty. How can I help you make this a success? Who can I introduce you to? What do you need? Where are the holes in your agenda?

How? What if...? How might we...?

. . .

SORRY, NOT SORRY

And while we are talking about unlearning certainty and saying hard things, we most definitely need to talk about the way we apologize and minimize. (Ladies, I am looking directly at you for this one.)

We need more wise, kind, and authentic leaders. We need them on stages and at the tables where decisions are being made. We need more diversity of thought and experience. And we need more mentors who are willing to tell their stories.

And yet when I reach out to make introductions, the first thing I am often met with is the wrong kind of certainty. The kind that makes people say, "I don't think I can do it. I don't think it's my place. I don't think I am good enough. I don't think I am ready."

Worse yet, these wise and wonderful leaders immediately minimize their abilities, using my least favorite word in the world: *just*. "Oh, I am *just* getting started. I *just* don't think I am ready. I am *just* a mom. I am *just* a secretary. I *just* don't think I am all that. I *just* don't think I have that much to contribute." It makes me want to scream.

Even when we are on stage holding the mic, or sitting at that table, the first words out of our mouths minimize our worth: "This might not be a good idea, but... Can I ask a dumb question? I don't have as much experience with this, but... Can I maybe offer an idea? Does that make sense?"

And then once we do show up bravely and put our work into the world, we sit back and apologize for it! "Sorry to be a bother. Sorry to ask you, but... Sorry, I got so emotional back there. Sorry, I just care too much. Sorry for being so passionate about this."

Years ago, my leadership coach gave me homework, and now I am passing it on to you. Every time one of these statements comes out of your mouth, I want you to punch it in the throat with some curiosity. Ask yourself:

What if you are ready? What if you are capable?

What if you are at that table or on that stage for a reason?

What if you aren't too much but instead are exactly enough?

What if you are in exactly the right place at exactly the right time to offer your unique perspective?

What if you have the power to change the world?

Because guess what? You *do*.

We should be having these conversations with each other more often. Look for moments to celebrate when colleagues speak up, own their capabilities, and show up with curiosity. Get a cake and turn a meeting into a party when your team takes a risk or asks, "What if?" instead of caving to certainty.

As Elizabeth Gilbert said, "Curiosity only does one thing, and that is to give. And what it gives you are clues on the incredible scavenger hunt of your life."

Curiosity is the turn on The Authenticity Map where you pick up momentum. If you can harness it, it will propel you and your team forward through whatever you face.

SELF-ASSESSMENT
• • •

What Do You Need to Unlearn?
- In what areas have you been applying certainty instead of curiosity?
- In what areas are you spending time planning when you should be doing?
- How can you apply curiosity to the ways you give and receive feedback?
- How can you walk toward disagreement with a sense of curiosity?

Get Started
Curiosity can be fun! And let's be honest—we spend way too much of our lives at work for us to not have fun there too. What if you tried Brad Montague's elementary school experiment on your own team? (You don't have to sit in a circle on the floor, I promise.) What if you asked your team the same questions about the people and customers you serve?—"I wonder who we could help? I wonder what is the most amazing thing we could do for them? I wonder who could help us?"

Imagine what this might unlock for you. Imagine how this approach might change engagement, collaboration, innovation, and communication for your team. You might be surprised at how far a little curiosity can take you.

CELEBRATE!

Bear with me on this one... I want you to celebrate sorting your mail. Learning to let go of the voices that aren't productive, meaningful, helpful, or kind can free us up to really pay attention to the feedforward that we need to grow. The next time you launch something, pay close attention to the responses you can let go of and celebrate the process of giving your attention to the right things.

REJECTION

● ● ●

Carrying around a list of everyone who
thinks you're not good enough is exhausting.

SETH GODIN

NOT EVERYTHING you say or do or create will be welcomed. Learning to speak up and approach your work with curiosity will lead to feedback—and some of it won't be positive. In fact, some of it will be flat-out rejected. How do you keep going when others reject you or your ideas?

This is a tricky roadblock because it's guaranteed to happen. And when it does, it's tempting to crawl right back into that failure mindset. *(I suck. Everything sucks. It will always suck.)*

But you know the way out of this now. There's no need to start at Go. Remember:

Do what you know.
Ask for help.
Curiosity over certainty.

My friend Jessica Swesey had fantastic advice about rejection. She said, "You know, I do this thing sometimes. When I start to wonder why anyone would ever want to read what I'm writing, I go on Amazon and read the reviews of Pulitzer Prize–winning books. It reminds me that even this book that literally won a Pulitzer Prize, there's some woman named Joanna who's like, 'This was terrible and never should have been written.' It's a nice reminder that everybody has a critic, and every piece of work is going to have people who reject it completely. Just because you've been deemed an award-winning writer doesn't mean everyone is automatically going to love what you're doing. If I could teach my kids one lesson about rejection, it would be that it doesn't mean anything."

No matter how amazing your work is, there will always be someone who rejects it completely. The most important reminder here is—don't let that person be *you*.

I once had a coaching call with a brilliant leader. She had a seat at the table because she had intelligent insights and deep experience. But she wasn't sharing her ideas. I asked, "What is holding you back?"

She didn't hesitate. "I am holding me back," she said. "I never speak unless I am certain I have the right solution. I weigh all the options of what they might think or say before I speak."

I knew where she was coming from. As a child, I was told over and over again, "We have two ears and one mouth, so you should listen twice as much as you speak." It was drilled into me to think first, then speak. And somewhere along the way that thinking turns to *What will they say? What if they hate it? What if they criticize me? What if they think I'm stupid?*

We talked about how to turn that thought process inward. To ask ourselves, "What do *I* think? Is this what *I* believe? Do *I* think my message is valuable?"

Putting our work into the world is a powerful thing. The value of our work shouldn't be determined by the hypothetical voices of others. There will always be a critic. There will always be someone who rejects your ideas. Don't let those voices hold you back . . . drown them out with your own. And then speak.

6

ANGER AND COMPASSION

THERE IS NO WAY TO DO THIS WRONG

• • •

To be angry is very good, I think. Anger is like fire:
it burns things out and leaves nutrients in the soil . . .
We should always be ready to be angry at injustice.

MAYA ANGELOU

THE AUTHENTICITY MAP

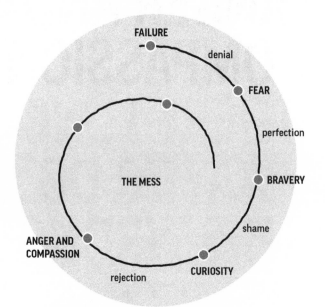

MANY YEARS ago, I attended a silent writing retreat held at a former convent over a four-day weekend. The goal was to live and write in silence all day, then come together in the evenings to share our writing with the group. My room was as austere as you would expect a convent to be. A twin bed, a desk with a wooden chair, and a small bedside table with a lamp. And on the bed, a single white index card with eight words on it: *There is no way to do this wrong.*

Most of the pages I wrote that weekend weren't very good. And it would be years before I turned them into something great. But that index card has sat on my desk ever since, reminding me of the most important lesson that weekend taught me: *There is no way to do this wrong.*

In marketing, it's a common approach to use the collective narrative. We say that everyone loves this one particular brand of cereal, or everyone is buying this purple toothpaste. Nine out of ten dentists recommend it!

It's a powerful strategy because it works. The desire to belong is a fundamental part of human nature. So fundamental that Maslow included belonging as one of the five critical human needs in his hierarchy, along with physiological needs, safety, self-esteem, and self-actualization. Countless scientific studies have found that belonging is linked to our sense of identity, mental and emotional well-being, and self-esteem.

However, we grow up with mixed messages about belonging and the collective narrative. On one hand, I'm sure you can hear your mother's voice ringing in your ears, warning you not to do stupid things just to fit in. (I can still hear mine asking, "If all your friends jumped off a bridge, would you jump too?") On the other hand, there was immense peer pressure to do whatever it took to fit in.

In my day, fitting in was all about whether you had the right bangs or whether the mean girls let you sit with them. But these days, our brains are running on digital crack cocaine, fed fifteen-second bursts of dopamine by an algorithm that is constantly dripping trending topics and audio clips. We are told we have to be exactly this or exactly that. Fitting in has never felt so complicated.

The collective narrative shows up at work as well, but it comes most commonly in the form of "everyone" and "always": *Everyone* is saying this. *Everyone* believes, feels, or wants a certain thing. It's *always* this way, it's *always* been this way, it will *always* be this way. There is no way all of those "everyone" and "always" statements can be true, but our brains are so wired to belong that we can end up running ourselves into the ground trying to meet unreasonable ambitions. It's an impossible way to lead others, and it's an even more unrealistic way to live ourselves.

The truth is, work is messy and hard. Leading others is messy and hard. Life is messy and hard. And no matter how brave or curious we get, things are still going to be messy and hard. This messy middle stage is where many of us get stuck and discouraged: "I did the work! I showed up and I bravely put myself out there! I asked the questions and approached things with less certainty. Why is everything still so damn hard?"

When I started working on The Authenticity Map, this chapter was supposed to be solely about compassion. I spent weeks trying to make that emotion fit here. I tried to write about making things nice, neat, and tidy—sort of like that ridiculous cafeteria tray.

"Just give yourself grace!" I wrote. "Let yourself off the hook. Stop scoring your efforts against an impossible set of goalposts." As if there was a simple Pinterest quote that could help us hop right through this messy middle part.

But the more I wrote, the angrier I got. Until one day, I found myself venting all of my frustration and anger on a group of my friends. I jumped on our shared Marco Polo thread and just let it fly.

"I'm so frustrated! I feel like I'm constantly tamping down and folding up and putting away!" I said. "We climb our way out of failure and fear and start showing up bravely and boldly. But then we are supposed to dial it back? I don't want to be quiet and small! I don't want to suffer in silence. I don't want other leaders to suffer in silence either. Enough of the suffering! Let's just solve the freaking problem!"

And then it hit me: *The emotion that also belongs here is anger.*

We are leaving failure behind. We're facing our fears. We're being brave and doing hard things. We become leaders with influence. But the world is telling us to "be professional." We are left asking, "Why am I keeping silent about the things that matter? Why am I dialing it back? Why am I trying to make everybody happy? Why have I come this far only to shove all the rest of my emotions into a box and stomp on them? Why am I playing small?"

Because the story we've always been told is that anger is bad.

"Keep your anger in check," they say. People who get angry at work—especially women—are perceived to be unstable, irrational, or out of control. There are a million articles about how anger is detrimental to our reputations or can harm our ability to be promoted. Heck, "The Angry Woman" is an entire stereotype. Heaven forbid we ever get angry.

Anger is always painted as a negative emotion, but what if anger is a good and healthy part of leadership? What if anger is exactly what we need to get from fear to joy?

I had been wondering why I was so angsty at this stop on the map, until it dawned on me that the map was saying, "You can't skip the anger. How do we lead with all of the emotions except anger? That's ridiculous."

And that is when my dear friend Meg Rector told me something so true and wise: "We have to include anger because anger means that we care. We care about the injustices, the places where people are being treated unfairly, the problems that need solving, all of it. We are angry because we see those problems. *You have to go through anger to get to compassion.* That is why compassion alone feels so anemic—because we haven't actually dealt with the firework that is burning inside of us."

When I started digging into why I was skipping the anger, all those deeply ingrained emotions about belonging rushed back. I thought, *I can't get angry! Is that even professional? What if I tell people what I really think? What if I call out things I think are wrong? What if I (gasp) say no?! What if I am that Angry Woman?*

I was skipping the anger because I was afraid my anger would make me stand out. That I would be different from the rest. That the collective narrative of "everyone" and "always" wouldn't apply to me.

And guess what? *It won't.* And that, my friends, is exactly the point. And that is when I remembered: *There is no way to do this wrong.*

* * *

GOOD ANGER

When I think back on the times in my life and career when I have been the most angry, it has almost always been because I believed with all my heart that something was very wrong. A line had been crossed or an unethical decision had been made.

Anger is a boundary-setting emotion. It allows us to say no. To draw a line in the sand and declare, "I won't do that. I won't stand for that. That's not right." It allows us to turn feelings of frustration or helplessness into action.

I remember the first time I led from anger. I was a freshman in high school, and my biology teacher was a scumbag. He made passes at the female students, gave higher grades to the ones that wore short skirts, and constantly made suggestive comments. The entire class felt the ick, and we talked about it in the halls, but we were a bunch of thirteen- and fourteen-year-olds. What were we supposed to do? Finally, after months of this, I'd had enough. I went to the office and asked to meet with the principal.

I recall feeling sick to my stomach. My knees shook and my palms were sweaty. But I sat in that office and I told the truth. More than thirty years later, I don't remember what the principal said, or what happened to the teacher. But I clearly remember my anger, and I remember what it felt like to *do something* about something. It felt freeing. It felt empowering. And it felt real. Not stifled or performative. And in that moment, I learned what good anger was.

As the old saying goes, "We teach people how to treat us." But I would amend that to "We teach people how to treat us *until we know better*." It can take us years of lessons to learn how to adequately set boundaries and use our anger for good.

But we can't lead others to set boundaries when we haven't learned to set them for ourselves.

Recently, I found myself in the position of president of my homeowners' association. I put my hand up because no one else did and, frankly, because I underestimated the boundary-setting that would be required. (Take note: if you are lacking boundaries, this role will either kill you or gift you hella boundary-setting skillz.)

If leading in this capacity has taught me anything, it's that I can't please everyone. It isn't possible. There are times I simply have to say no, take a stand, and do what I think is best for everyone that I am serving.

In the case of one particular neighbor, that wasn't good enough. When a decision was made that he didn't like, he became like a dog with a bone. The messages were incessant, and they grew increasingly hostile, bullying, and personal. For months I told myself that this was what I signed up for—this was part of the job. But I grew more angry as time went on. I would vent about him to my friends, stress about his messages as I was falling asleep, and replay my decisions in my head, becoming angrier as each day passed.

• • •

You have to go through anger

to get to compassion.

• • •

Until I realized I wasn't angry at him—I was angry at myself. I hadn't set boundaries for myself. As a result, there wasn't any clarity around expectations or communication, because the people around me didn't know where those boundaries were.

As soon as I set boundaries (*this is accepted behavior, this is not, and this is how I will respond in both circumstances*), my anger disappeared. His behavior didn't change in the slightest. But now I could respond (or not) without the guilt or stress.

Anger isn't bad. It's a normal and natural emotion. It comes down to what we do with that anger, whether we take positive steps forward or whether we allow it to fester and hold us back.

Good leaders don't make decisions *with* anger, but they often make decisions *from* anger. Making decisions with anger can leave us feeling even more angry and stressed. We keep the anger within us and it fuels our actions. Decisions made with anger can feel retaliatory, instead of clarifying, and can leave others feeling punished instead of led.

But decisions made *from* anger give us freedom. They allow us to call out the things that need to be brought into the daylight and make those around us feel seen, heard, and guided. Even when they may not agree with the decision. That day in the principal's office, I was acting not *with* anger, but *from* anger.

No matter how brave and curious we are, no matter how many boundaries we set, we are still guaranteed at some point to hit a wall of conflict. We won't agree with everyone and everyone won't agree with us. Our point of view or values won't align with everyone all the time. We will even have to lead people who have vastly different views or opinions. "Everyone" and "always" simply isn't a thing.

Learning to use good anger and lead from it in times of conflict makes all the difference. It's time to unlearn the lie that anger is bad. Anger can be one of the most productive emotions we can experience—and it can play a critical role in conflict resolution.

Anger can motivate us to take action. Researchers have discovered a link between anger and what's known as approach-related motivation. This is the idea that two main forces drive our behavior: the impulse to move toward things we want and the impulse to move away from things that make us uncomfortable.

Surprisingly, scientists at Texas A&M found that anger significantly activates the left cortex of the brain, which makes us move forward toward discomfort. In contrast, fear and sadness activate the right cortex, which is linked to inhibition, caution, and avoidance.

This means that when you're angry, your brain is essentially giving you a boost of energy and motivation to take action or address challenging and unfair situations. It's like your brain's way of saying, "Let's do this!" even in the most uncomfortable situations.

Anger can make us happier. I know what you're thinking on this one, but bear with me. Harvard researcher Dr. Jennifer Lerner, who studies emotion and decision theory, found that anger was associated with optimism and risk-taking, whereas fear was associated with pessimism and risk aversion. Additionally, angry people are more similar to happy people in how they assess risk outcomes.

Lerner found that leaders who employ good anger are more likely to take more risks and have more positive outcomes, because when we are angry, we can feel more optimistic about our ability to change a particular situation. This empowers us to more confidently take action.

Anger can increase cooperation. Anger can help make our teams stronger and better when we use it the right way. A study from the Society for Personality and Social Psychology found that sometimes it's necessary to talk honestly and get a little angry to solve a problem. If we're angry for a good reason, and we express it in a helpful and appropriate way, it can clear up misunderstandings and disagreements. When we express our anger, it can lead to more cooperation and understanding. This might feel uncomfortable in the short term, but it can make the relationship healthier in the long run.

It's so interesting that anger, motivation, boundaries, and action all seem to travel together. Whereas suppressing our anger only seems to lead to staying stuck, fearful, and miserable. When messy moments happen at work, anger can be an immediate reaction. But if we act *from* anger, instead of *with* anger, we can set appropriate boundaries, have clearer conversations, solve problems faster, and promote more cooperation. (And be happier at the same time!)

• • •

YOU ARE NOT FOR EVERYONE

I think we turn the corner from anger to compassion when we find our true selves. I used to think that I had to be like someone else to be doing it right. I had to lead like the leaders I once had. I had to coach like the coaches I observed. I had to twist myself like a pretzel to belong in those rooms, on those stages, and at those tables.

Looking back, I think it was the collective narrative that I got stuck on. *Everyone* and *always* left me feeling like there was only one way to be, only one way to succeed, and only one way to lead.

Until that point, I had been believing the lie that I not only had to aspire to be like everyone else, I had to aspire to do the same things better. But the quest for *same only better* was killing me. It was sucking my soul and keeping me from being the friend, leader, teammate, and human that I was supposed to be. And truth be told, I didn't like myself very much. It had never occurred to me that the reason might be because I wasn't actually being me.

And then one day, I heard Sally Hogshead take the stage and say these words: "Different is better than better." And a lightbulb went on in my life.

She was right, and my old approach hadn't been working. So I started doing things differently.

Ken Black, a brilliant creative director with over twenty years of experience with Nike, says when we hedge our bets and play it safe, people can feel it. When we play it safe in life or our work, we stop short of who we truly are because we are afraid to take a point of view. Ken often reminds us that the legendary sneaker designer Tinker Hatfield once said, "If people don't love or hate your work, you just haven't done all that much."

The idea of people hating our work can be terrifying. The idea of being different can be terrifying. The idea of not fitting in or belonging can be terrifying. But the thought of going through our entire lives or careers trying to fit in by being *same only better* is the most terrifying thing of all.

When we take off the mask and start showing up as our real selves, when we take a point of view or a stance that others may not agree with, or when we use our good anger to take action, there are going to be those who don't love it. The pool of people who are fans and followers is going to narrow. And that is totally fine. Because the pool of people who love you, love your work, and who will follow you anywhere is going to be much, much richer. As Ken says, "In the end, you want to make something beloved. Don't be afraid to have someone hate what many others love."

You are not for everyone. And thank goodness, because that would be exhausting. You can't possibly please everyone. But pleasing, serving, or leading anyone well when you aren't willing to be different is nearly impossible.

Authenticity is going to feel like the most freeing thing ever once you give up the idea of *same only better*. It's going to feel like the last day of school. Like whipping off your bra at the end of the day. Like jumping into the lake on the hottest day of summer. Suddenly, your good anger is going to make sense, because it's not a barrier—it's a driver. It's moving you from fear into compassion and joy. That left cortex of your brain is going to light up like a freaking Christmas tree, y'all!

That good anger is going to cause you to push back against what is not right, shine a light on the shadows, and help you create things that people are going to love. It's going to break your heart and fire you up and show you who you are and who you are not. That good anger has a purpose. It tells us exactly why we are here and what we are supposed to do about it. And suddenly, we start to understand the people around us better. We look at our teams, colleagues, and clients with fresh eyes, recognizing that their emotions are the road map to their hearts and minds.

Fitting in has always been about following the rules that others have set for us. But belonging happens when we make our own rules and people come alongside, saying, "Yes, me too!" Real authenticity begins when we realize that we can *not* fit in and still belong.

It begins when we can let go of the idea that we have to look or act a certain way to be taken seriously. Or that we have to lead with the same tactics we were exposed to.

For me, while it might seem silly, it meant realizing I could wear Chucks on stage instead of heels and my message was just as important and impactful. I can coach with empathy and emotion, not just with KPIs and goals. For me, different really is better than better.

* * *

SUFFER TOGETHER

Sally Zimney, a bravery expert, bestselling author, and dear friend once wisely told me, "If I want to be a truth-teller, I need to let my anger fuel me to share what is really inside of me and what I truly believe about the world. Sometimes that will make others feel uncomfortable and I won't always be the nicest freaking person in the room."

We often have this crazy idea that we can't get angry about things. We have to be "nice" and "good" and "professional"—and those things are mutually exclusive from anger. But nothing will ever change unless somebody gets angry about something.

Anger and compassion are two sides of the same coin. They are both passion.

Passion means *to suffer*. Compassion means *to suffer together*. (From the Latin *com-pati*—"suffer with.") Anger is passion *for* something. Compassion means to suffer *with* others.

Anger is an emotion we have toward something. But compassion isn't a feeling—it's an action. We *have* anger, and because of that anger, we *do* compassion.

We have to suffer for what we care about. And then we have to suffer *with others*. That is the point of leadership.

We must become truth-tellers and sometimes make people uncomfortable in order to do the right thing. And then we have to do that *with* the people we lead, empowering them to do the same.

The whole idea behind leading from anger and doing compassion is that we are willing to suffer for something that's worth it. And most importantly, to suffer with others. Together. As a team.

I think back to my friend Brad Montague and his analogy of leadership as a shipwrecked sailor (Chapter 3). The role of a leader is to steady the boat, consult the compass, and find the wind. But the very best leaders bring shipmates along with them. Leaders don't go it alone.

Just as we can't go it alone in fear, we also can't go it alone in anger.

Research has shown that when we act compassionately, our heart rate slows, we produce the bonding hormone oxytocin, and the regions of the brain linked to empathy, caregiving, and feelings of pleasure light up, which can result in our wanting to care more for others. And that also makes us feel better about ourselves. In short—suffering together leads to belonging.

• • •

Just as we can't go it alone in fear,

we also can't go it alone in anger.

• • •

The collective narrative of *everyone* and *always* is an impossible thing to live or lead up to. The idea of *same but better* is a recipe for exhaustion and burnout. But if we can learn to be fueled by our good anger and suffer together by doing compassion, we can create teams where no one fits in but everyone belongs.

SELF-ASSESSMENT
● ● ●

What Do You Need to Unlearn?
- What collective narrative has been holding you back in your work?
- What boundaries are you missing?
- Are you focused on *same but better*? In what ways are you willing to be different?
- How are you modeling compassion for your team? In what ways are you suffering together for the things that matter most?

Get Started
This can be a major turning point on your journey to authenticity. I know it was for me. Let go of the things you think you are supposed to be, and start using your good anger to move you forward. It will fuel you to face discomfort and choose to be different. This will free you up in ways you can't even imagine. Enough playing small. It's time to show up bigger, braver, and bolder. These are the moments when you take risks together, and your team truly becomes a team.

CELEBRATE!

I know this sounds a bit odd, but celebrate your anger. What fires you up? What breaks your heart? What gives you hope? How are you using those emotions to fuel you and form your point of view? The next time you or a team member has strong emotions about something—pay attention. It might just be an indication of an area of growth or opportunity. Those emotions will attract others who feel the same, and bring about stronger and more effective points of view in your work.

COMPARISON

• • •

We won't be distracted by comparison
if we are captivated with purpose.
BOB GOFF, author of *Love Does*

T HE WOMAN showing up in my Instagram feed was very fancy. Her hair was perfectly straight—not an unruly curl in sight. Her crisply pressed suit was definitely not hastily ironed in her hotel room. She wore six-inch heels without a sign of pain or discomfort. And I didn't know a dang thing about her before I made up an entire story in my head.

I immediately assumed she had her stuff together and was better than me at everything. I started looking at all of our differences and silently making lists in my head of all the ways I didn't measure up. In a matter of minutes, I had determined that she was amazing and I was not, and because I was nothing like her I was never going to succeed at anything, so I might as well give up. The end.

The comparison spiral is one hell of a drug, friends. There is a reason they call it the thief of joy. This roadblock is the fastest way straight back to failure and fear. Do not pass go, do not collect $200. Of all the stops on The Authenticity Map, this one can be the trickiest to get past. But we simply cannot get to joyful, authentic leadership if we spend all our time comparing our progress to others.

Comparison is a normal, human response. We are inherently social creatures. We naturally focus on what other people are doing. It's tough to simply ignore others all the time, especially people we work closely with. So, how do we move past this roadblock?

Know thyself. We all have our triggers. For some of us, it's social media. For others, it's obsessing about the people we compete with for roles or opportunities. Recognizing what is most likely to kick off the comparison spiral will allow us to see it for what it is. Some triggers we can avoid, others not so much. But being able to see them for what they are is the first step.

Exercise that muscle. For most of us, beating the comparison spiral is something we have to work at. It takes consistent and intentional practice. We can all stand to be more consistent about positive self-talk and intentional gratitude. Being purposefully grateful is a super powerful way to stay focused on our own journey.

You are not for everyone. (*No one is.*) It can be tempting to slide back into those old habits of *I suck, everything sucks, it will always suck* when we see others excelling. Remember—you are not for everyone, and that is perfectly fine. There is no one way.

The collective narrative is a big, fat lie. And you are more likely to find your people and your joy when you are focused on differ-ent, not *same but better.* Thank goodness there is room on this planet for all the flavors of ice cream! Just as there are people out there who love vanilla, there are plenty of people looking for the exact flavor that you are.

Gather shipmates. I remember once complaining to a friend about all the things a colleague had accomplished by my age. I went on and on about how they had done this and that. Finally, my friend looked at me and said, "Okay, people we are not comparing ourselves to: that person." When you find yourself spiraling—reach out. Don't go it alone. Most of the time, the fastest and easiest way to break out of a comparison spiral is to have someone else give you a swift reality check.

Eyes on your own yoga mat. We can't create and destroy at the same time. It's hard to focus on the things we are doing and accomplishing when we are busy talking ourselves out of them. Compete with your own dang self. Buckle down and work on your own goals. Stay so focused on your purpose that you don't have the energy left to look around.

Shabnam Mogharabi laughingly told me, "A friend once told me that the best advice they were given is to keep their eyes on their own yoga mat. I love yoga and I particularly love hot yoga. But every time I go, I'm always like, *Why is that person upside down on their head in a tree pose on one hand, and I can barely do the downward dog correctly?* When you're in a yoga studio, it's easy to be like, *What's happening with the contortionist over there when I can barely touch my toes?*"

(Y'all, I *feel* that.)

She continued, "I always feel so good after yoga. Even if all I did was downward dog, I come out sweaty and cathartic. And so, when my friend said that to me, I was like, 'You're right. Life is a yoga class.' It feels so good at the end when you've been able to do your touching of the toes and your downward dog. But if you constantly stare at the contortionist in the corner, you're just never gonna go to the class. Comparison prevents you from taking the first step and the next step. But taking that first step puts you on a path to feeling so good and finding joy."

At the end of the day, we are always comparing our insides to someone's outsides. It's not a fair comparison. Everyone has their own set of issues and insecurities. Perfection is a myth. Look how far you've come, friends. Eyes forward. Keep going.

By the way, that perfectly pressed blonde woman with high heels? I finally met her in person, and she was far less perfect than I had imagined her to be. She came with her own backpack full of hang-ups and insecurities. We all do.

7

CONFIDENCE
GOIN' ON
A BEAR HUNT

• • •

We're going on a bear hunt.
We're going to catch a big one.
We're not afraid.
It's a beautiful day!
AMERICAN FOLK SONG

THE AUTHENTICITY MAP

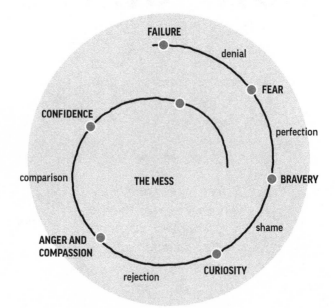

REMEMBER THE day like it was yesterday. It was a cold spring evening and I was leaving the office for the last time. After nearly twenty years working in a corporate setting, I had resigned. I carried a cardboard box filled with the contents of my desk through the doors and out into the wide world of self-employment.

Standing in the parking lot that evening, I was equal parts excited and terrified. I'd always left a role with another one lined up. But this time I was starting my own thing. I had no backup plan. No safety net. And no idea if I was going to be able to pay my mortgage. But I had one thing—I knew the only way forward was through.

Jason Jaggard, CEO of Novus Global, once described these realizations as "Ariel Moments," referencing *The Little Mermaid*. When we are in a situation, a job, or an organization, and we want more. More opportunity, more responsibility, more being seen, more passion, more joy. But the people around us keep saying, "Wait. Slow down. Be patient. Sit still. You aren't ready yet."

Sometimes we have to leave, Jason says, because our story has to be told somewhere else. In those situations, the choice isn't to stay or go: it's stay or *leave and grow*. Just like seeds are not meant to stay tucked in the ground and never grow into the light, we are not designed to be comfortable—we are designed to grow. Comfort rarely leads to growth, and the most successful people find comfort in being uncomfortable.

I was leaving a really comfortable gig. A nice office. A great boss. A generous salary. A group of colleagues I enjoyed working with. But I had spent several years hiding in my tent, pitched firmly in failure, fear, and denial. And that day I spent sobbing in the utility closet was a turning point. I realized that I was never going to move forward toward joy and become who I was meant to be if I stayed comfortably miserable. I had reached the point where I wanted more.

As a child, I looked forward all year to the week I went to sleepaway summer camp. It was a chance to be free of chores and siblings, and simply be. But the part I loved the most was when the sun went down and we gathered around a campfire, telling stories, and singing songs. My favorite camp song has always been "We're Going on a Bear Hunt."

For those not familiar with this song, it describes the journey of, well, going on a bear hunt. Each verse describes a different terrain—tall grass, a big river, squishy mud, a dark cave—and the way to navigate it. Spoiler alert: there's only one way. As the song goes, "We can't go over it. We can't go under it. We gotta go through it." Ironically, each verse also includes the line "We're not afraid"… until we find the actual bear in the cave and do the whole trek in reverse at top speed.

The truth is, I had been a liar. I'd been speaking about bravery, risk-taking, and comfort zones for years, but I was doing the complete opposite—both in my role as a leader and in my personal life. I had been living in that comfortable tent of failure and denial, refusing to move or grow. I was a big, fat chicken. My marriage fell apart, my life was a mess, I was in a deep depression, and I refused to believe it or accept it or speak about it. Instead, I just denied and preached the same stuff like some sanctimonious goody-goody. And I was miserable.

Until I reached the bear in the cave, so to speak.

For me, that "bear" was the realization that I could do this forever. I could fool everyone around me forever. I could paste on a smile, do the job, be miserable, and stay comfortable *forever*. And frankly, that scared the snot out of me.

I took a good look at my life and my career and decided I wanted more than comfortable misery. I wanted joy. And in order to get there, I was going to have to make some changes. I was *gonna have to go through it*. For me, that was the start of walking (sometimes crawling) my way through The Authenticity Map—a map that helped me navigate the messiest of emotions and finally figure out how to be truly authentic.

* * *

CONFIDENCE DEFINED

Confidence is not something we find all of a sudden. For many of us, it's not even something we are born with. It's something we build as we grow, brick by brick. For me, it was the biggest and boldest step toward joy. Daring to be myself, to set boundaries, to speak up, and to be brave was only part of the journey. Confidence meant I had to show up and lead.

A few years ago, I read an article that Mindy Kaling had written about her book *Why Not Me?*, and this paragraph touched a nerve.

> When I started at *The Office*, I had zero confidence. Whenever Greg Daniels came into the room to talk to our small group of writers, I was so nervous that I would raise and lower my chair involuntarily, like a tic. Finally, weeks in, writer Mike Schur put his hand on my arm and said, gently, "You have to stop." Years later I realized that the way I had felt during those first few months was correct. I didn't deserve to be confident yet.

I found myself reading that a few times, circling the line *I didn't deserve to be confident yet.* I remember thinking, *Deserve?* Deserve? I had never thought of confidence as something I had to earn or deserve. It kind of rubbed me the wrong way. I thought about it for weeks. Do some people deserve confidence and others don't? What does one even have to do to deserve confidence? (And if Mindy doesn't deserve it, is there any hope for the rest of us?)

To this day, I am still not sure if I think confidence is something we do or do not deserve, but I do know it's something I had to become friends with. It didn't come naturally to me. Bravery was easier because I was doing the thing, but I was doing it scared. Doing something with confidence felt audacious. Loud. Showy. All the things I had been raised not to be. All the things I had been told that good girls aren't.

(Can I just say how refreshing it is that younger generations are hearing much healthier messages? I love seeing the youths embracing their voices boldly, loudly, and bravely. Confidence isn't radical for them; it's ingrained. And I am Here. For. It.)

Definitions can sometimes trip us up. As my coach and mentor Harris III likes to remind me, I can sometimes build this entirely false definition of something in my head. (Guilty as charged.) "Confidence" is one of those words. We commonly mistake it for its cousins—"ego," "entitlement," and "arrogance."

Ego operates out of self-interest. It seeks approval, praise, and validation at all costs in order to be seen as right.

Entitlement expects others to do things for it because it is owed something. Entitlement most often comes from unreasonable expectations.

Arrogance believes it knows it all and refuses to accept help. It has an inflated sense of itself and can't see that it might benefit from the advice of others.

Confidence means having faith in your own abilities. Confidence is based on trust in ourselves and in those around us. Confidence is knowing that you are capable even when you don't have all the answers or experience. It can be far tougher to have confidence—because while ego, entitlement, and arrogance don't care if they are right, confidence knows it might not be and has to show up anyway.

I had to work to make friends with this emotion. To trust that I could step up and lead others, even while I was still learning and felt uncomfortable. And that was the whole point—confidence isn't always comfortable. Leadership isn't always comfortable. Getting uncomfortable is how we grow.

The interesting thing was, by the time I got to the confidence stop on The Authenticity Map, I already had everything I needed to step up.

I had learned to fail with purpose, to fail forward, and to allow myself to step back without deduction.

From fear, I learned to tell the truth and ask for help.

. . .

Confidence is knowing that

you are capable even when you don't

have all the answers or experience.

. . .

Bravery taught me to stop worrying about what things look like from the outside, to focus on what I know, and to ask for what I want.

As curiosity replaced certainty, I learned to give and receive feedback, speak up, and take action even when the path wasn't totally clear.

And *from* good anger, I learned to *do* compassion.

I had all the tools. I might not always have the answers or the experience, but I have the ability. That is confidence in a nutshell. Confidence is what allows us to reach joy and authenticity. It's the piece that snaps it all into place. And when we fully lean into it, it feels like a freaking celebration.

Let there be cake! It frees us up to be exactly who we are and do exactly what we are meant to do. And it gives us the fuel to do some of the toughest parts of leadership.

. . .

SAYING NO

Saying no is something we all struggle with. It's funny because statistically, as children, this is the word we hear the most often. It's usually the first non-familial word we learn to say. And as children, we throw it around with abandon. But as we grow older, we learn that saying no is not always popular. It's difficult. It gets challenged. And for many of us, we eventually just stop saying it altogether.

There are many reasons we might have trouble saying no:

We want to avoid confrontation.

We want to be helpers and make other people happy.

We have a case of FOMO.

We are compulsive yes-sayers.

We honestly think we can take on all things and do all things.

If you want joyful work, you need to have the confidence to say no. And I'm not just talking about the easy no. It's not that hard to say no to the things we genuinely don't want to do. I am talking about the times when we have to say no to things that are awesome, the opportunities that we really want, and the things that sound like fun.

We know when things don't align with our goals. And no matter how much we'd love to go down every rabbit hole, there are some opportunities that simply don't align. Setting clear priorities and alignment is one of the most important roles of a leader.

A leader establishes the answers to these questions:

Why does our company/organization/team exist?
How do we behave?
What do we do?
How will we succeed?
What is most important right now?
Who must do what?

This list is the compass you consult before you set your sails. It's the North Star that keeps you and your shipmates aligned. The flip side of each of those questions, of course, is the no.

How do we *not* behave?
What *don't* we do?
What is *not* most important right now?

If we aren't saying those nos, it's impossible to keep everyone aligned.

Saying no allows us to set boundaries (which we talked about in Chapter 6). When we don't set boundaries for ourselves and our team, we let someone else's boundaries run the show. As much as we may not want to let someone down by saying no, we have to remember that allowing our team to be off alignment is letting them all down.

My doctor once told me that saying no has an important effect on our brains. When we learn how to say no more easily, we alter the way our brain thinks and reacts, giving us the ability to make quicker and better decisions. This doesn't just have a positive impact on our leadership; it allows us to trust ourselves more, which makes us more confident in our abilities. Saying no is yet another brain muscle we have to exercise. (It all comes back to the brain, doesn't it?)

• • •

SAYING YES

Every time we say no, we are saying yes. Every time we say no, we are making a choice. If it's no to this, then it's yes to that. All too often we focus only on how challenging it is to say no, and we forget about the yes on the other side. Compared to the no, saying yes feels like it might be the easier path. But when it comes to taking risks, that's not always the case.

Years ago, I was asked to transition from a role I loved into a role that came with more of everything—more money, more responsibility, more autonomy. From the outside, it looked like an easy yes. But I turned it down. Three times, actually. Until the president of the company took me to lunch and asked me personally to take the job.

That was the hardest yes I ever made. I knew what it was going to lead to. I knew it would push me and stretch me and take me far, far outside my comfort zone. I knew it would teach me more lessons than I could imagine about leadership, people, and relationships. I knew it would bring so many positives into my life. But I also knew that one day, it would lead to me standing in the parking lot, holding the contents of my desk in a cardboard box.

We have to say yes to the challenges that will change us. We have to say yes to the opportunities that will push us out of our comfort zones. Even if they ultimately lead to Ariel Moments.

I have learned if it's not a clear yes, then it's a clear no. If it's not a hell yes, it's a hell no. There are times that will clearly call for one or the other, and neither will be easy. Say both, confidently. Mean it. And then adjust your sails.

● ● ●

GOING ALL IN

Rebecca Campbell wrote in *Light Is the New Black*, "The world is filled with people who, no matter what you do, will point blank not like you. But it is also filled with those who will love you fiercely. They are your people. You are not for everyone and that's OK. Talk to the people who can hear you. Don't waste your precious time and gifts trying to convince them of your value, they won't ever want what you're selling. Don't convince them to walk alongside you. You'll be wasting both your time and theirs."

The day I fully accepted that I am not for everyone was one of the greatest days of my career because it freed me up to go all in on being who I *am* for. I had to let go of some people in my life and career to make this adjustment, and this is one of the greatest and toughest results of confidence— we'll disappoint some people. We'll leave some people behind as we grow. But we'll attract others who will cheer us on, push us forward, pull up chairs for us, and advocate for us.

Being not for everyone might mean that you care more about what you believe in and your purpose than about what others think. This can feel selfish and contrary to the way you were raised. (It certainly did for me.) Being not for everyone might mean that you stop catering to the unhappy minority in order to better serve the engaged majority.

In every group I speak to, there is always at least one heckler. One person who usually sits in the back of the room with their arms crossed, making it crystal clear that I am *not for them.* When I started speaking, I used to focus on that one person. I would turn cartwheels to try to win that one person over, instead of focusing on the other ninety-nine people in the room. I was convinced I could get them to come around. Until one day, when a speaker feedback survey was sent to me with the comment "Spent more time on the one guy who was never going to get it than on the rest of the group." Gulp!

At that moment, I realized that "the one guy" wasn't my audience. He came with his mind already made up that he didn't want to learn or change. Trying to win him over or convince him wasn't just a waste of my time; it was robbing those who *were* my audience of a fully present and authentic me. There is always going to be that one guy. He is not your audience. I can water down who I am, what I believe, and what I bring to the table to try to make everyone moderately happy, or I can bring my talents, ideas, and experiences as they are and make some people stand up and cheer.

Our goal is to be the perfect choice for someone, not just an okay fit for everyone. Go all in, friends. Show up authentically every time.

• • •

STEERING THE SHIP

It's our job as leaders to get everyone on our team playing for the name on the front of the jersey, not the name on the back. Or to continue the ship metaphor—keep them all rowing in the same direction. This was one area where I had to lean hard on confidence. I didn't always have the answers. (I still don't. I never will.) When I first became responsible for leading others at work, I made a million mistakes. But I knew I had the ability. And I had some fantastic mentors along the way.

Elizabeth Kuhn was one of those mentors. "EK," as we called her, came into my career like Mary Poppins—a whirlwind of much-needed medicine paired with a spoonful of sugar. Dynamic, energetic, fun, and telling it like it was. As the VP of promotions and education at an international brand, EK was made the captain of a group of people that were spread all over the globe, on a ship that had half a sail and was taking on water. Over the next few years, her leadership turned us from a scattered group of people into a well-oiled team that had a vision, a North Star, and the confidence to lean all the way into our individual strengths. EK single-handedly shaped the way I came to view myself as a leader and taught me some critical lessons on ship steering.

Keep it balanced. If everyone leans to one side, at best, you row in circles. At worst, the ship sinks. Every member of the team has to stay focused on their own tasks, but they have to work together. If they don't communicate, they'll find themselves rowing in circles endlessly. Expensive mistakes are most commonly made when teams are competing amongst themselves, rather than working together.

Plug the holes. Every ship is going to spring a leak now and then, but one of the worst moments as a leader is finding that a member of your own team is drilling holes in your boat when you aren't looking. I once hired a bright young man as a member of my team. He had so much potential. He was smart, driven, and likable. But he was driven by ego and entitlement, as opposed to confidence. We found that he was stealing from the company, and not only did I have to fire him, we also sued him for theft and breach of contract. To this day, he is still the biggest disappointment of my career. But the lesson EK taught me in that moment will stand out as one of the most important. She said, "The way people treat you is a statement about who they are. It is not a statement about you. Shit will always happen that you can't control. Plug the holes and move forward."

Know your lighthouses and lifeboats. Storms are going to come. Every team will experience them. A good ship's captain will know when it's time to steer for shore or abandon ship. Every lesson in this book that applies to leaders applies to our teams as well. It's our job to empower the people around us to navigate their own journey to authenticity. On the day I found myself sobbing in the utility closet, EK was the one who joined me there and gave me the nudge I needed to jump ship. A poor leader might have tried to keep me on board and comfortably miserable, but EK knew it was time to leave and grow. A truly great leader knows that they have to craft the space for their people to be uncomfortable enough to grow within the team they have. But they also need to know when it's time to let someone go.

Keep an eye on the weather. EK was always really great at keeping us from getting overwhelmed. She kept an eye on the workload and wasn't afraid to put herself between us and a difficult client or situation. A great leader keeps an eye on the weather and prepares their team in advance for coming storms. But they also know that in good weather, there should be time to rest, recover, and stockpile for the rough times.

When I called EK to chat about this chapter, she said, "I have become much better in recent years at making sure that the efforts my team is putting into something moves our goals forward. So I don't feel guilt if we say no to a random RFP [request for proposal] on something that I know at the end of the day doesn't move the brand forward. If it's not helping move the brand forward, I'm over the guilt of saying no.

"I used to say, 'Well, we have time, right?' And we might very well have had the time to do something for someone else. And it might be a priority for them. But it has to keep to the 80/20 rule. If 80 percent of our work is purposeful and productive in moving us forward, great. But that doesn't mean that the 20 percent has to be filled with random things that are constantly keeping us overwhelmed."

She went on, "I used to always try and fill the cracks because it was helping somebody. But what if we used that 20 percent space to just breathe and think, or put together a book club with the team so that every call doesn't have to be crammed with to-dos and miscellaneous projects?

• • •

Our goal is to be the perfect choice

for someone, not just an okay fit for everyone.

• • •

"We can then get to a place where we say, 'Okay, we're through our workload. Let's talk about the chapter we all just read that will help us grow as humans, will help us grow together as a globally spread-out team, and will help us do our jobs better.' We can build culture when we're not constantly filling the 20 percent with the small stuff just to fill a schedule. It opens doors to other things."

I owe a lot of my career lessons to EK, and this last lesson might just be the most important. She taught me that work is about culture and joy, not just an endless list of tasks to check off. When I think of EK, I remember most the moments of celebration and tears. The emotion of being human, real, and authentic. She taught me (and continues to teach me) how to bring my humanity to work, and I am a better ship's captain because of her.

• • •

TAKING UP SPACE

For many, this is one of the trickiest parts of stepping into confidence. It can feel the most anti-all-the-things-we've-been-taught or anti-the-lies-we've-been-told. But it can be the most fun. This is the part where we show up and cheer for ourselves. We take up more space. We own our mess. We live out loud. We do the hard things in the daylight. This is the part where we refuse to self-deprecate. We stop being our worst critics and instead be our own biggest fans.

Look at how far you've come, friend! Look at how you have left the failure, fear, and denial behind and embraced bravery and curiosity. Look at how you are bringing passion and confidence to the table—while setting that table for others too! You are doing the hardest work of all—you are becoming a truly authentic leader. You aren't buying those BS rules anymore about leaving your emotions at the door; you are using them to show up exactly as you are.

You can only lead people as far as you are willing to lead yourself. It's impossible to create and lead authentic, creative, curious, and confident teams if you aren't willing to show up that way yourself. I didn't have the confidence to own my mess when I was in the utility closet. But once I did, everything changed. I learned to own my weird, say no, and take new risks that I never would have otherwise taken.

You are capable, even when you don't have all the answers or experience. Remember, confidence isn't always comfortable. Leadership isn't always comfortable. Comfort is the enemy of growth.

We can't go over it. We can't go under it. We gotta go through it.

SELF-ASSESSMENT
• • •

What Do You Need to Unlearn?
- Where are you remaining in comfort when you should instead be growing?
- What is keeping you from saying no?
- Are you focused on being a perfect fit for someone or an okay fit for everyone?

Get Started
It's time to start putting all those lessons to the test. You have the ability; now it's time to believe you have the capability.

In what areas are you holding back? Where can you use your confidence to move from comfort to growth? You don't have to quit your job. (Or maybe you do. Only you know.) But you do need to start showing up fully as yourself, taking up space, and empowering those around you to do the same.

How are you spending your 80/20? If your 80 percent is moving you forward, what is filling that 20 percent that is uncomfortable enough to help you grow?

CELEBRATE!

I want you to celebrate finding out who you *are* for and finding out who you are *not* for. This can sometimes feel like an un-fun process, so let's celebrate it instead! One of the first things I did as a business owner was identify my ideal audience. I made an actual list. Who are they? What do they struggle with? What do they need? What do they want? What are they afraid of? The more I got to know who I was for, the more excited I became. They are out there, they need what I have to offer, and there are so many of them!

I became so focused on the people I am for, I stopped obsessing about the people I am not for. They didn't disappear. They still show up in my inbox sometimes or in the audience with their arms crossed. But I know how to sort my mail and stop turning cartwheels now. I can say no when I need to. And I am confident I have something awesome to offer. Friends, *that* is worth celebrating.

ROADBLOCK

EGO

●　●　●

The greatest leader is not necessarily the
one who does the greatest things. He is the one
who gets the people to do the greatest things.

RONALD REAGAN

HAVE SEEN many leaders get stuck in this roadblock for
much of their careers. They work all the way through The
Authenticity Map but never quite make it to joyful authenticity. It's sad to watch, honestly. But ego is a sneaky thing.
It sometimes looks exactly like confidence. They are cousins,
after all. But while a confident leader says, "Look at us!" a
leader stuck in ego says, "Look at me!"

I get why this is a sticking point. The literal definition of a
leader is someone in front. At the head of the line. At the top
of the list. Maybe this is why I have had such a complex relationship with the term "leadership" for much of my career. I
genuinely believe anyone can lead, and you don't need a title

to do it. And I believe it is the job of leaders to create more leaders, not to simply amass a bunch of followers.

The very best leaders are often not the single face of the organization or the single voice of the brand. Nelson Mandela once described this kind of leader as a shepherd, saying a good leader "stays behind the flock, letting the most nimble go out ahead, whereupon the others follow, not realizing that all along they are being directed from behind."

There are three key reasons why shining the spotlight on our teams, rather than on ourselves, leads to more authentic and joyful leadership.

It motivates. Genuine praise becomes addictive. The more we feel appreciated, the more we want to earn more of it. It makes us feel good, and we are motivated to keep feeding our brains that good feeling. Leaders who take the approach of "Look at me!" instead of "Look at us!" or, even better, "Look at you!" are going to find that their teams are less motivated to contribute, put in extra effort, or stay on the team at all.

It serves others. Leadership is all about the art of giving. Great leaders know that guiding others means serving them. Acknowledging and giving credit to others shows gratitude, and gratitude is the key ingredient to building trust and loyalty. True leaders value collective triumph more than individual praise and are always looking for ways to show appreciation to their team. Joyful and authentic leaders make generosity and appreciation a daily practice.

It's scalable. Perhaps the best reason to avoid the ego roadblock . . . it's really difficult to be all things to all people. Leaders who take the "Look at me!" approach soon find that they are facing burnout, exhaustion, teams that don't work well together, and they struggle to grow and scale.

I once was presenting a strategic plan to the leadership team, and I repeatedly referred to a collective "we." I said things like "We plan to accomplish this and this by Q4" or "We'd like to see these kinds of results this year."

Puzzled, one of the VPs stopped me and asked, "Isn't it just you in your department, currently? Who is 'we'?"

I remember laughingly replying, "Oh, well, I always use 'we.' It's just me right now, but I work together with all of the departments and it's never just me accomplishing things."

Ultimately, that attitude led to more responsibility and opportunity for me, but it also allowed me to grow a team that felt the same way. We were able to have more impact and serve more people because we shared a collective rallying cry of "Look at us!"

Ego is self-serving. But truly joyful leaders serve those they lead. They are constantly building a backbench or a farm team. Knowing that when it's not all about them, they can serve more people, create happier teams, and bring more of their ideas to life.

8

JOY
SET THE
TABLE

• • •

It's all such a mess,
and in the middle of the mess
we still somehow make beauty,
and in the middle of that beauty,
we still somehow find joy.

BRANDI KINKAID, artist

THE AUTHENTICITY MAP

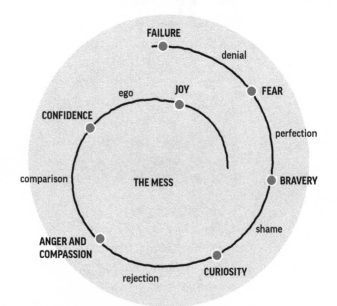

HAVE ALWAYS been fascinated by the story of Sir Ernest Shackleton.

Ernest was born in 1874 in Ireland, the second of ten children born to Henry and Henrietta Shackleton. He had an obsession with adventure from an early age and was particularly inspired by the stories of polar explorers such as Roald Amundsen and Robert Falcon Scott.

He was a restless and unfocused student, and in 1890, Ernest left school at just sixteen and joined the merchant navy. By the age of twenty-four, he was certified as a master mariner, qualifying him to command a British ship anywhere in the world.

In 1901, Ernest joined Scott's British National Antarctic Expedition aboard the *Discovery* as third officer. The expedition reached a record southern latitude, coming within just five hundred miles of the South Pole, but was forced to turn back due to a lack of supplies (and scurvy and frostbite).

He married. Had kids. Became a politician. But never lost the yearning to conquer the Antarctic.

In 1907, he tried again. The *Nimrod* Expedition came within ninetyish miles of the Pole and made some important scientific discoveries. But the entire crew nearly starved to death.

He came home a hero. Was knighted. Had another kid. And in 1912, he learned that another expedition had finally done it—they had reached the Pole. This is when Ernest hatched his biggest plan yet.

The *Endurance* Expedition, also referred to as the Imperial Trans-Antarctic Expedition, was launched in 1914 with the goal of crossing the Antarctic continent from sea to sea. It would be a grueling eighteen-hundred-mile trek on foot across mostly uncharted land. The expedition was made up of two ships, fifty-six men, seventy sled dogs, and a (male) cat named Mrs. Chippy.

The journey would stretch out to nearly three years and end in what most would consider utter failure. The *Endurance* became trapped in the ice and was crushed, eventually sinking. Ernest and his crew were forced to abandon the ship and take to the lifeboats. They traveled over thirteen hundred miles across the Weddell Sea to South Georgia island, where they were eventually rescued.

There is an urban legend that before the *Endurance* Expedition, Ernest placed an advertisement for crew that stated: "Men wanted for hazardous journey. Low wages, bitter cold, long hours of complete darkness. Safe return doubtful. Honour and recognition in event of success."

While the existence of this particular ad has never actually been proven, it is true that Ernest received over five thousand applications to join the voyage.

Over five thousand men (and reportedly two brave women) volunteered to go on a journey where they were basically promised failure and death. *Why?*

If any elements of the ad are true, I am guessing these weren't the draw. And reports show that the "low wages" bit wasn't an exaggeration. Most of his crew never got paid, and Ernest himself died deeply in debt.

But the most interesting thing about Ernest, for me, has always been the stories about how he chose his crew. He didn't hire his men solely for their necessary skills like carpentry, meteorology, and science. He hired based on morale.

It's said that Ernest believed that character was as important as technical ability, so he chose people who could sing and play instruments. He also promoted camaraderie by distributing the ship's chores equally among officers, scientists, and seamen. And he socialized with his crew members every evening after dinner, leading sing-alongs, jokes, and games.

I have a hunch that people didn't sign up for low wages, bitter cold, and near-certain death. I think they signed up for the joy.

• • •

JOY REDEFINED

Plenty of people use the terms "happiness" and "joy" interchangeably, but for the final stop on The Authenticity Map, I use the term "joy" on purpose. They are two different things. Linked, but different.

Happiness is tied to external factors, so your happiness is impacted when things go wrong (you burned dinner, lost out on a promotion, or spilled coffee on your pants). But joy is an internal feeling. It comes from being at peace with who you are, what you have achieved, and what you are capable of.

Happiness is affected by the circumstances that surround us. Friendships, travel, holidays, memories—they can all lead to a feeling of happiness. But you can still have joy when things are not going your way. When you have joy, it's easier to be happy. But it's much more difficult to find happiness if you don't have joy. Joy lasts longer than happiness ever will.

You will never be able to control all the stuff that happens to you: your business, your team, or your family. You'll face failures, setbacks, fears, and disappointments. You will have unhappy times. But you can still have joy. You can still be joyful.

Shabnam Mogharabi says, "Happiness is an emotion, like anger or fear. It comes and it goes. When you find twenty dollars in your pocket when you're doing the laundry, you're like, 'Score, today's gonna be a good day.' That's happiness. It comes and then an hour later you might feel another feeling. Joy, however, is an internal point of view that you have. It's a set of tools, a set of skills, that allow you to have a different perspective on what comes your way. So you can find joy in sadness. You can find joy in happiness. You can find joy in fear. Because it's about the perspective that you're bringing to something and the set of tools you're able to pull from."

I know, I know, I'm getting dangerously close to going full woo on you right now. But trust me, I know what I'm talking about. Throughout my journey around this map, I have had many unhappy moments. My marriage fell apart. I had to move. We experienced a global pandemic. My business went through extreme low points. But as I learned these lessons and became more authentically me, I found joy. And eventually, I chose joy. Joy in work, and joy in life.

Joy forced me to look inward and find the best parts of myself. It gave me purpose and was a bright light at the end of the tunnel. Joy became the reason I kept going. Because once you feel the difference between joy and happiness, you want more joy. You can't get enough. Joy is the result of being exactly who you are meant to be, doing exactly what you are meant to do.

. . .

Joy is the result of being exactly

who you are meant to be, doing

exactly what you are meant to do.

. . .

I can't imagine that nearly dying from scurvy and frost-bite was happiness-inducing. I can't imagine that living on a tiny wooden ship with smelly men and dogs for months (or years) was always happy. But I can understand completely the joy that comes from believing in a purpose so much that you are willing to forego your happiness to achieve it.

Joy plays a significant role in our leadership journey. If we create teams that are always chasing happiness, we are going to struggle. Every setback or mistake will send us into a tailspin. But if we can learn to choose joy, and teach those around us to do the same, we'll create teams that are unstoppable, even when it feels like the world is coming down around us.

Let's look at three instances in particular where joy can make all the difference.

When we make mistakes. We are all going to make them. Our teams are going to screw things up. Perfection isn't a real thing and we are going to have failures and setbacks. All. The. Time. In these situations, joy is going to give us purpose and direction. It will remind us to follow the map— fail with purpose, move forward, ask for help, do what we know, and ask better questions.

Joy keeps us moving forward when we make mistakes because we have a purpose. We are all working to sail the ship in the same direction. If we were all chasing happiness instead, we'd all be furiously rowing in different directions.

When we need to change. Ooof. Who loves change? Honestly, most of us don't. Again, we can blame our brains for this one. Change naturally releases a cocktail of ingredients into our brains, the strongest of which is fear. But we can combat that with purpose, and this is what leads to joy. Anyone who has ever walked across coals will tell you that there is a point where you can turn off the fear portion of the brain and turn on the purpose portion. We go from "This might be awful" to "I must do this."

The fancy name for this switch is resiliency. The ability to continue on and move forward even when your brain is in the background saying, "Nope, not gonna do that!" Resiliency and joy go hand in hand. Change is a never-ending requirement. No matter what business you are in, it is guaranteed to change at some point. When we can lead our teams to become resilient and purposeful, we will all be more joyful, even amidst change.

When we need to own our weird. Years ago, when I started talking about being weird, I would occasionally get the odd look or the scrunched-up nose. Weird? People could get on board with being different, unique, quirky even. But weird sometimes felt like a bridge too far.

But I love the word "weird." It sounds like it is. Strange. Odd. Uncomfortable. And joyful. It breaks the rules. (*I* before *e*, in particular.) It's not a conforming word; it's a rebellious word. And I think it perfectly explains the way it feels to be authentic and joyful. When we get to this stage of leadership, it's going to look weird to others at times. People aren't always going to see the purpose that drives you, or even agree with it.

A great leader is going to have to own their weird. Stand behind the things they do that make others scrunch their noses. Our path is going to look weird to others who are not driven by purpose, authenticity, and joy. But that same purpose and joy is going to allow us to stay the course, even when it looks strange from the outside.

● ● ●

IT'S NOT YOUR JOB (OR IS IT?)

I used to think it was the job of a leader to help those around them find joy.

I asked Shabnam about this. She is so eloquent about joy and happiness. I wanted to know how she helps others find their joy. Her reply surprised me. She said, "I don't think it's anyone's responsibility to help other people find joy. I think joy is a tool you have to develop for yourself. But I think you can create an environment and a culture that allows people to do that."

She continued, "At SoulPancake, we had a 'no question is dumb' policy. We wanted people to ask questions. We told people, if you don't know what you're doing and if you feel like you are in over your head, we don't want imposter syndrome. We don't want people being like, 'I'm just gonna fake it till I make it.' Raise your hand and say, 'I don't know how to do this.' Because I would rather have an environment where people are stepping up to help you figure out how to navigate challenges rather than you trying to basically wade your way through it."

It is a leader's job to create a culture where everyone can find joy for themselves. Shabnam had brilliant insights on how to create an environment and culture that allows your team to develop joy and resilience.

Do a lot of postmortems. "Celebrate the wins—celebrate what went right. Talk about what could have gone better and do it in a way that isn't about individuals, but about process. This creates a culture of learning where you're always trying to improve, which motivates people to reflect on what they could have done differently and what they could have done better. At the end of the day, joy is just a series of self-reflections, right? It's about self-reflecting your way to a different perspective."

Don't take yourselves too seriously. Shabnam said, "Humor is used often in awkward situations or uncomfortable situations as a crutch, but I also think humor and levity can be used to change the way that we perceive challenges and problems. We never took ourselves too seriously and that was part of our culture. I think that was important for people to feel like they could be themselves, grow, make fun of themselves, make fun of situations, and not take things too seriously. Because at the end of the day, we weren't curing cancer. We were making videos to try to uplift people and get them to explore the human experience. It was meant to be thoughtful, reflective, and fun."

Don't dismiss the hard parts. "I think that there is a tendency when you're talking about joy to conflate it with optimism and cup half full. Joy is not about that. Joy is about embracing all of it and changing your perspective on it. It's about saying, 'Wow, that was a really hard project,' or 'Wow, that was a really challenging client.' And accepting that those things are true and you can still also find a way to approach them with a different perspective. A lot of my role as a leader was to cultivate a culture where joyfulness could thrive. But it was never my responsibility to make other people joyful. It was my responsibility to create a culture that would allow people's intrinsic joy to come out."

I love this unlearning so much. As a leader, I am not responsible for making you joyful. I am responsible for setting a table where joy is served and inviting you to pull up a chair. Things are still going to be hard or challenging. Everything isn't always going to go right. We aren't always going to have all the answers. But we will serve joy at this table, and we invite you to join us. What a beautiful way to look at our roles as leaders.

• • •

BEING THE BOSS

I have had bosses, and I have had leaders. They are not the same.

I once had a boss who would come into the office each morning, walk past everyone without saying a word, enter his office, and close the door. We were a relatively small group, only about twenty in total, and the space was open-plan. It was hard to miss this behavior day after day, and over time, it became a topic of conversation among the team. It affected morale and led to a sense of distrust.

After months of this, at an all-hands meeting, the boss asked the team to share any feedback on ways he could be a better boss. Hesitantly, someone mentioned that he could take the time to say good morning when arriving in the office. The boss looked genuinely surprised. He explained that he tried to time block his first hour every morning to stay focused and came in with the intention to not get sidetracked.

He listened as, one by one, we chimed in with how it made us feel ignored or unimportant. He was shocked. It had never occurred to him. He assumed we also wanted to time block our mornings or work undistracted. He had never imagined that it was having a negative impact on the group.

From that day on, each morning, he arrived and greeted us. He said good morning, asked how we were doing, and interacted with the team. Morale improved, our interpersonal relationships improved, and our relationships with him improved as well. But the truth is, morale didn't just improve because he said good morning. Morale improved because he asked us how he could improve, he listened to our feedback, and then he followed through.

Simon Sinek says, "A boss has the title. A leader has the people." Not all bosses are leaders. And not all leaders are bosses. It's wonderful when you can find someone who is both.

. . .

YOU ARE NOT YOUR TITLE

Speaking of titles, I have had more titles over the years than I can count. I find that each year, professional titles get a little more ridiculous. I met someone the other day whose title had *thirteen words* in it. I shudder to think of what that looks like on a business card.

We put a lot of emphasis on titles. Naming things is a kind of an obsession in the professional world. Often promotions are given in title only. Titles infer rank, power, opportunity, and places at the table. When we meet someone new, the second question most commonly asked is "What do you do for a living?" When someone is interviewed on TV, their occupation is listed below their name. It's no wonder that many of us can get stuck in the trap of thinking that our title defines us.

It would be a mistake to talk about leadership and joy and not talk about balance. It's the giant elephant in the room. After all, we aren't just talking about becoming joyful leaders. We are talking about becoming joyful leaders at *work*. Work—a thing we have to balance with the entire rest of our lives, which includes all of our other roles and titles. Parent. Friend. Spouse. Child. Volunteer. Cook. Cleaner. Person Who Must File Taxes. Let's face it—it's hard.

I think one of the lies we must unlearn is that there is such a thing as balance—at least, balance defined the way we've been told. Balance isn't a neat, tidy stack where everything has a place and it all fits perfectly. Balance, in reality, is a mess. And specifically, balance requires us to embrace the mess.

· · ·

Not all bosses are leaders.

And not all leaders are bosses.

· · ·

I love Shabnam's perspective on this. She says, "I think balance is a lie that we've been told, particularly as women, as mothers, as partners, as well as people in the workplace. It is a hundred percent a lie. I don't think it is possible to achieve work-life balance. The way I think about it is actually analogous to relationships. You know, people always say in a relationship that you want a fifty-fifty partnership. But the reality is that that's never true in any relationship at any given point. Someone is always taking on more than the other person."

She went on, "Now, you hope that ebbs and flows, right? That sometimes I need 80 percent of the time and the attention and the resources of our relationship, and other times I'm only gonna need 20 percent, right? Sometimes

80 percent of my needs are met, sometimes 20 percent of my needs are met, and that ebb and flow in a healthy relationship is normal. It is totally normal because nothing is ever fifty-fifty. It's just impossible to every single day be like, 'Did you do 50 percent of the chores? And I did 50 percent of the chores. Did you do 50 percent of the childcare? And I did 50 percent.' That's impossible."

OMG we laughed at this, y'all. I mentioned to her that I had recently heard Brené Brown describe fifty-fifty marriages as BS, and we laughed even more. The truth is, nothing is truly balanced. Not marriage, not leadership, not anything.

As Shabnam said, "There are gonna be ebbs and flows. I think with this weird misnomer we have of work-life balance that is also true. There are going to be times in your life when work consumes 80 percent of your time because you're building, you're trying to grow your career, to establish yourself. And there's gonna be other times when your career is only 20 percent of your attention because you have babies at home or you've got a sick parent. So that's just the nature of relationships, and I think that's the nature of the relationship between work and personal life too."

She went on, "I do think that we've been taught to silo our lives. We've been taught to say your work is here, your family is here, your health is here, your faith life is here, your sense of play and adventure is here. We're told to silo off all the little parts of ourselves, and at work there's just work persona, and that's all that shows up. But I think that's another lie we tell ourselves. I believe that the leaders who earn the respect and adoration of their teams are the leaders who have been able to break down the walls between their silos and are willing to not only say, 'This is me at work,' but also 'Here's me in my personal life, and here are the things that I struggle with both personally and professionally.'"

Yup. I felt the weight of my cafeteria tray as she said that. Silos aren't just a lie; they are downright unsustainable.

"It's really important to break down those silos and have that vulnerability," Shabnam said. "It creates so much loyalty amongst employees when leaders are vulnerable and open about their personal and professional challenges. We have to break down those silos that we put in our lives and acknowledge that work-life balance is not real. Sometimes you're gonna have more emphasis on work, sometimes more on life. That's just the nature of being a human."

Balance and joy don't fit in those tidy little cafeteria trays, friends. You are not your title. You are not defined by your title. You are not what you do. That is only a single aspect of who you are. I like to remind people that we are human beings, not human doings. (Or as the brilliant speaker Carrie Wilkerson says, "We are humans, *being*.")

Balance and joy come when you are in *purpose*. Goals, tasks, seasons, priorities—these will change. But your purpose will not. This is what defines you. Not your title.

• • •

THE JOY IS IN THE MESS

Ernest Shackleton chose his team not just because of their useful skills; he chose them based on what they would contribute to the journey. He chose as he did because he knew that the journey would bring hazards, darkness, and danger. They would face fear and failure, even death. But he also knew that they had a collective purpose. And to achieve their purpose, they would need to choose joy.

They would need to choose possibility in their grief. They would need to choose discomfort in their fear. They would need to choose bravery, curiosity, and passion. And they would need to believe they were capable, even when sailing into uncharted waters.

Ernest chose people who would be part of a team. They would work together, sing together, play games, and support each other regardless of the challenges they faced. They attempted one of the messiest and most disappointing expeditions of their time. They didn't achieve their goal. But they stayed true to their purpose—and not a single man died on the three-year journey. I'm guessing they didn't have cake, but I am sure in those three years, they celebrated their accomplishments. They survived by working as a team in some of the harshest conditions. And I have to believe that despite it all, they found moments of joy.

If you've been paying attention, you've realized that The Authenticity Map doesn't really end. Nor is it a neat and tidy circle. It sort of leaves you hanging in the mess. You might be thinking, *Is this it? I get to joy and then it's over? What now?*

Authenticity is a habit, not a destination. There is no end to the map because the work is never done. You'll have to start over and over again. It's only a short hop from joy to failure because one good screwup and you are right back where you started. Getting to joy is a daily practice that requires embracing all the emotions and navigating all of the roadblocks.

When we learn to navigate the mess, we can truly be authentic—not only as leaders but in all of the other roles life brings our way. There is no joy without the mess. You will always be messy. But you can be joyfully messy. That is the ultimate goal. Joy is not the end of the map, but once we learn that the joy is in the mess, *through* the mess, we'll spend less time on the journey each time failure shows up.

SELF-ASSESSMENT
● ● ●

What Do You Need to Unlearn?

- How do you define success? Do you simply look at the goals achieved, or do you consider the resiliency you are developing along the way?
- In times of failure or change, are you chasing happiness, or are you choosing joy?
- Are you allowing yourself the vulnerability to break down those silos that may be leading to unrealistic expectations and burnout?
- How are you defining joy as a leader? Is it a destination or a journey? Is this a definition you need to unlearn?

Get Started

So many of the steps on The Authenticity Map require us to examine the definitions we assign to the words we've long used. Success isn't just about ticking off boxes or marching toward KPIs. Leadership isn't necessarily about being the first in line. And joy isn't about pasting on a smile and faking it until we make it.

As you explore ways to implement these lessons and integrate this map into your own leadership journey, take the time to challenge the way you are applying definitions. Do you need to redefine joy, authenticity, and balance for yourself? Can you see where and when your team requires both a boss and a leader? Are we coaching our teams to be resilient, even when your purpose may seem weird or uncomfortable?

CELEBRATE!

Authenticity is a habit, not a destination! This is great news. It means we can let ourselves off the hook for not being there yet. Every day is another opportunity to work those muscles and get stronger and better. It's not our job to make those around us joyful. All we can do is set a table, put joy on the menu, and show people the map. It's up to them whether they come aboard or pull up a chair. Those who do are going to make this journey so rich and wonderful. That feels like something worth celebrating.

WE'RE GONNA NEED CAKE

● ● ●

HERE IS a reason the word "celebrating" is in this book's title.

I started my journey sobbing in a utility closet. I pitched my tent in failure, denial, and fear, and lived there for a very long time. My life was messy and I was too. And for years, I thought there was no way out. That I was going to have to fake it and fool people into believing I had my life together forever. Because I believed the lie that we can't be messy AND... It was exhausting.

Then came the day when I realized that the mess was never going to go away. That we are all messy—but the joy is in the mess. That day I took the first step toward navigating my mess, learning as I went that if we wait until we are not messy, we'll never do anything. We won't lead that team, climb that mountain, start that company, get on that stage, or achieve that goal. We'll just sit in our mess and misery forever.

Those first steps were scary. But they were progress. And over time, that progress became more and more noticeable to me and to those around me. My steps became quicker and lighter, my stories became more hopeful, and the light at the end of the tunnel became bigger and brighter. And I was able to bring others along with me.

I love to use cake as a metaphor, but the truth is, the cake simply stands for the moments of humanity with your team. A common thread throughout The Authenticity Map is not going it alone. Recruiting shipmates, gathering others—this is the ultimate celebration of leadership.

• • •

If we wait until we are not messy,

we'll never do anything.

• • •

When I think back to all the best cake moments in my career thus far, I wasn't celebrating alone. My team was in the trenches or at the table together, figuring it out, digging in, and supporting each other.

These days, life is still messy. The world is messy. And work is messy. I don't have all the answers, and I don't always know what to do.

But I have a map. And now, so do you.

I don't think we celebrate our journey nearly enough. I don't think we pause often enough to look back and celebrate how far we've come. I don't think we celebrate the small things enough.

I don't just want you to be joyful, authentic leaders.

I want you to unlearn the lies and replace them with the messy, joyful truth.

I want you to disturb the universe.

I want you to live out loud.

Fail forward. Rebelliously risk.

Gather shipmates.

Own your weird.

And set a table where joy is served for anyone who wants to pull up a chair.

I want you to find the kind of joy that makes you want to stick a fork in a chocolate sheet cake and eat it for no reason other than to celebrate being your very own messy self.

Authenticity isn't the absence of mess. You will never not be messy. But you can be messy AND...

And that is worth celebrating.

ACKNOWLEDGMENTS

• • •

THIS BOOK never would have happened without the support and encouragement of so many dear humans. I will be eternally grateful to my Marco Polo girls, the Poetics Guild, Elizabeth Kuhn, Marc Pimsler, Katie Burke, Shabnam Mogharabi, Nichole Bundschuh, Brad Montague, Tom Kuiper, Pottery Lane, Valerie Alexander, Dan Coughlin, Jessica Swesey, and Firefly Creative Writing.

I am so grateful to those who have come before me, allowing their stories to shape my life: Sheryl Sandberg, Brené Brown, Kim Scott, Scott Monty, Jon Acuff, Marianne Williamson, B.T. Harman, José Andrés, Glennon Doyle, Elizabeth Gilbert, Sally Hogshead, Jen Hatmaker, and Jason Jaggard.

All my love to my mama, for always making sure I keep moving toward joy.

And for my grams, for teaching me what a life well lived looks like.

For Maple, for keeping me company.

And for H, always.

NOTES

• • •

Chapter 1: The Mess: Ditch the Cafeteria Tray

"personality rather than something that can be taught": Scott
    Monty, "That Which We Are, We Are," *Timeless & Timely*,
    September 20, 2023, timelesstimely.com/p/that-which
    -we-are-we-are.

they perform better when they can be themselves at work:
    Liz Villani, "The numbers behind the need for change,"
    Be Yourself at Work (podcast), August 23, 2023, pages.be
    yourselfatwork.com/byaw-global-survey.

In Canada, those results were one in four: Institute of Health
    Metrics and Evaluation—Global Health Data Exchange
    (GHDx), "Depression," accessed March 7, 2024, vizhub
    .healthdata.org/gbd-results/; CIGNA U.S. Loneliness Index,
    May 2018, cigna.com/static/www-cigna-com/docs/about-us/
    newsroom/studies-and-reports/combatting-loneliness/
    loneliness-survey-2018-full-report.pdf; Heather Gilmour
    and Pamela L. Ramage-Morin, "Social isolation and
    mortality among Canadian seniors," Statistics Canada
    Health Reports, June 17, 2020, doi.org/10.25318/
    82-003-x202000300003-eng.

loneliness a "priority public health problem": WHO, "Social
    Isolation and Loneliness," accessed February 16, 2024,

who.int/teams/social-determinants-of-health/demographic
-change-and-healthy-ageing/social-isolation-and-loneliness.

destabilizing teams and organizations en masse: Wikipedia,
s.v. "Great Resignation," last modified March 7, 2024,
en.wikipedia.org/wiki/Great_Resignation.

equal to 11 percent of global GDP: Gallup, "State of the Global
Workplace: 2023 Report," accessed March 7, 2024, gallup
.com/workplace/349484/state-of-the-global-workplace.aspx
#ite-506924.

". . . what employees experience in your work culture every day": Jake
Herway, "Need an Answer to Quiet Quitting? Start with Your
Culture," Gallup, October 24, 2022, gallup.com/workplace/
403598/need-answer-quiet-quitting-start-culture.aspx.

Chapter 2: Failure: Don't Stick the Landing

"a story of overcoming adversity to actually get there": Christine
Wang, "Mary Lou Retton: Ignore your critics, do what you
love," CNBC (website), April 8, 2016, cnbc.com/2016/04/07/
mary-lou-retton-ignore-your-critics-do-what-you-love.html.

It's always going to suck: Steven F. Maier and Martin E.P.
Seligman, "Learned Helplessness at Fifty: Insights from
Neuroscience," *Psychological Review* 123, no. 4 (July 2016):
349–367, doi.org/10.1037/rev0000033; Martin E.P. Seligman,
Learned Optimism: How to Change Your Mind and Your Life
(New York: Pocket Books, 1991).

failure "an essential prerequisite" for success: Yian Yin, Yang
Wang, James A. Evans, and Dashun Wang, "Quantifying the
dynamics of failure across science, startups and security,"
Nature 575 (October 2019): 190–194, doi.org/10.1038/
s41586-019-1725-y.

people who didn't have to do anything to get in: Elliot Aronson
and Judson Mills, "The effect of severity of initiation
on liking for a group," *Journal of Abnormal and Social
Psychology,* 1959 (2), 177–181, doi.org/10.1037/h0047195.

"not to let failure be the last thing you do": Howard Tayler, Schlock
Mercenary (website), September 18, 2017, schlockmercenary
.com/2017-09-18.

Chapter 3: Fear: Do It Scared

"slowly moving us toward the magic": Meera Lee Patel, *My Friend Fear: Finding Magic in the Unknown* (New York: Penguin Publishing Group, 2018).

"Learn from fear but don't let it lead": Jon Acuff, LinkedIn, accessed March 10, 2024, linkedin.com/posts/jonacuff_someone-committed-to-fear-will-not-be-converted-activity-6920774504944193536-8vqA?trk=public_profile_like_view.

"it's that we are powerful beyond measure": Marianne Williamson, *A Return to Love: Reflections on the Principles of "A Course of Miracles"* (San Francisco: HarperOne, 1992).

"the belief that you are worthy of a big life": Kristin Lohr (@kristin_lohr), Instagram, accessed March 10, 2024, instagram.com/p/BwkG85_hlTT/?utm_source=ig_web_copy_link&igsh=MzRlODBiNWFlZA%3D%3D.

"'Yes, disturb the universe, disturb it!'": Madeleine L'Engle, "Dare to Be Creative" (speech delivered to the Library of Congress), November 16, 1983.

Roadblock: Perfection

GETMO *stands for "good enough to move on"*: Craig Groeschel, "GETMO: Good Enough to Move On," Global Leadership Network (website), September 26, 2019, globalleadership.org/videos/leading-organizations/getmo-good-enough-to-move-on?locale=en.

"The purpose is to make your work better": Seth Godin, "Show your work," *Seth's Blog*, March 17, 2016, seths.blog/2016/03/show-your-work/#:~:text=You%20should%20ship%20when%20you,to%20make%20your%20work%20better.

Chapter 4: Bravery: Pull Up a Chair

"Eat in the kitchen, / Then": Langston Hughes, "I, Too" (originally named "Epilogue") in *The Weary Blues* (New York: Opportunity, 1925).

"Life punishes the vague wish and rewards the specific ask": Timothy Ferriss, *Tribe of Mentors: Short Life Advice from the Best in the World* (New York: Harper Business, 2017).

negotiation as appropriate and even necessary: Linda Babcock
and Sara Laschever, *Women Don't Ask: The High Cost of
Avoiding Negotiation—and Positive Strategies for Change*
(New York: Bantam, 2007).

"Black women's 63.1 percent, and White women's 79.6 percent":
Institute for Women's Policy Research, "Equal Pay Day 2022:
Despite wage gains in recent months, women still earn
just 83 percent of what men make across most sectors and
occupations," March 15, 2022, iwpr.org/equal-pay-day
-2022-despite-wage-gains-in-recent-months-women-still
-earn-just-83-percent-of-what-men-make-across-most
-sectors-and-occupations/.

"Your playing small does not serve the world": Marianne
Williamson, *A Return to Love: Reflections on the Principles of
"A Course of Miracles"* (San Francisco: HarperOne, 1992).

Roadblock: Shame

"douse it with empathy, it can't survive": Brené Brown, "Listening
to Shame," TED Talks, March 2012, ted.com/talks/brene_
brown_listening_to_shame?hasSummary=true.

"empathy and understanding, shame can't survive": Brown,
"Listening to shame."

Chapter 5: Curiosity: Saying Hard Things

(At least until the next book.): H.A. Rey and Margret Rey, *Curious
George Rides a Bike* (Boston: Houghton Mifflin, 1952).

it will increase risk and lead to inefficiency: Francesca Gino,
"The Business Case for Curiosity," *Harvard Business Review,*
September 1, 2018, hbr.org/2018/09/the-business-case
-for-curiosity.

They just start cooking: "Our Story," World Central Kitchen
(website), accessed March 10, 2024, wck.org/story.

"all you can do is react to that turn": José Andrés, *The World
Central Kitchen Cookbook: Feeding Humanity, Feeding Hope*
(New York: Clarkson Potter, 2023).

Does this sting because it is true and important and real?
   Glennon Doyle, Facebook, April 21, 2020, facebook.com/
   watch/?v=226416608462952.

believed their managers provided such feedback: Nicole
   Abi-Esber, Jennifer E. Abel, Juliana Schroeder, and
   Francesca Gino. "'Just Letting You Know...': Under-
   estimating Others' Desire for Constructive Feedback."
   Journal of Personality and Social Psychology 123, no. 6
   (December 2022): 1362–1385, doi.org/10.1037/pspi0000393.

"creates relationships able to weather the storms": Patrick Thean,
   *Rhythm: How to Achieve Breakthrough Execution and
   Accelerate Growth* (Austin: Greenleaf Book Group, 2014).

"disagreement is what gives an organization vitality": Megan Reitz
   and John Higgins, "Title overview" of *Speak Up: Say What
   Needs to Be Said and Hear What Needs to Be Heard* (New
   Jersey: Financial Times Publishing, 2019), pearson.com/
   en-ca/subject-catalog/p/speak-up/P200000004457/97812
   92263014.

Chapter 6: Anger and Compassion: There Is No Way to Do This Wrong

which is linked to inhibition, caution, and avoidance: Eddie
   Harmon-Jones, Philip A. Gable, and Carly K. Peterson,
   "The role of asymmetric frontal cortical activity in emotion-
   related phenomena: A review and update," *Biological
   Psychology*, September 4, 2009, apsychoserver.psych.arizona
   .edu/jjbareprints/psyc501a/readings/Harmon-Jones%20
   Gable%20Peterson%20Bio%20Psychology%202010.pdf.

This empowers us to more confidently take action: J.S. Lerner and
   D. Keltner, "Fear, anger, and risk," *Journal of Personality and
   Social Psychology*, 81, no. 1 (July 2001): 146–159,
   doi.org/10.1037/0022-3514.81.1.146.

it can make the relationship healthier in the long run: Society for
   Personality and Social Psychology, "Sometimes expressing
   anger can help a relationship in the long-term," August 2,
   2012, sciencedaily.com/releases/2012/08/120802133649.htm.

"Different is better than better": Sally Hogshead, website homepage, accessed March 19, 2024, sallyhogshead.com.

suffering together leads to belonging: Dacher Keltner, "The Evolutionary Roots of Compassion (video)," *Greater Good Magazine*, July 2012, greatergood.berkeley.edu/video/item/ dacher_keltner_the_evolutionary_roots_of_compassion.

Chapter 7: Confidence: Goin' on a Bear Hunt

"I didn't deserve to be confident yet": Mindy Kaling, "Mindy Kaling's Guide to Killer Confidence," *Glamour*, August 4, 2015, glamour.com/story/mindy-kaling-guide-to-killer -confidence.

"You'll be wasting both your time and theirs": Rebecca Campbell, "You Are Not for Everyone," *Rebecca's Blog*, rebeccacampbell .me/you-are-not-for-everyone/.

Chapter 8: Joy: Set the Table

leading sing-alongs, jokes, and games: F.A. Worsley, *Endurance: An Epic of Polar Adventure* (New York: W. W. Norton & Company, 2000); Wikipedia, s.v. "Ernest Shackleton," last modified February 18, 2024, wikipedia.org/wiki/ Ernest_Shackleton.

("We are humans, being."): Carrie Wilkerson, website, accessed March 19, 2024, carriewilkerson.com/.

ABOUT THE AUTHOR

• • •

VALERIE GARCIA is a speaker and coach on a mission to move organizations from fear to forward. With methods that challenge the traditional, she uses her straightforward style and sense of humor to encourage her clients to lead with joy and think outside the box when it comes to connecting with their customers. In her over twenty years' experience, she has worked with entrepreneurs and companies, such as RE/MAX, Berkshire Hathaway, HubSpot, and Duke University, on six continents. Garcia will help you celebrate change, take bold risks, and embrace the power of your messy authenticity. She lives in Grand Rapids, Michigan.

DEAR READERS,

It's time to *move*. The Authenticity Map is waiting for you! Are you ready to take your business, team, or organization from fear to forward? Let's celebrate change together.

GET MOVING.

Find out more about how to guide others through The Authenticity Map. Get bonus resources at valeriegarcia.com/cake.

INVITE ME TO SPEAK.

My keynotes, coaching, and workshops are known for their sense of humor and nuts-and-bolts style, motivating audiences to get real and take action. I've worked with organizations around the globe to help them face fear, fail forward, and find joy in the mess. Inquire at valeriegarcia.com.

GET MY LOVE LETTER.

If you've enjoyed this book, you'll love my newsletter. It's delivered each month to thousands of leaders just like you. It's full of stories, tools, and lessons that will inspire you to lead authentically. Sign up at valeriegarcia.com/loveletter.

SHARE THIS BOOK.

If your team or organization would benefit from reading this book, I'd love to hook you up with a bulk order. For information on bulk purchases and discounts, contact orders@pagetwo.com.

CONNECT WITH ME.

I want to hear how this book and The Authenticity Map have helped you! Drop a review on your favorite online retailer's website, or slide into my DMs.

Facebook/LinkedIn/Instagram @valeriegarciaspeaks